Your marketing sucks.

Your marketing sucks.

Mark Stevens

CROWN
BUSINESS
NEW YORK

Grateful acknowledgment is made to the following for permission to reprint previously published material:

John & Chris Corelli: "Corham" ad. Reprinted by permission of John & Chris Corelli.

Crimson Technologies, Inc.: "Destruction Unlimited" ad. Reprinted by permission of Crimson Technologies, Inc.

Mazza: Two "Synergy" ads. Reprinted by permission of Anthony Mazzei.

Power Quest Corporation: "Cognet" ad. Reprinted by permission of Power Quest Corporation.

Stark & Stark: "Stark & Stark" ad. Reprinted by permission of Stark & Stark.

Published by Crown Business, New York, New York.
Member of the Crown Publishing Group, a division of Random House, Inc.
www.randomhouse.com

CROWN BUSINESS is a trademark and the Rising Sun colophon is a registered trademark of Random House, Inc.

Printed in the United States of America

DESIGN BY BARBARA STURMAN

Library of Congress Cataloging-in-Publication Data
Stevens, Mark, 1947–
     Your marketing sucks / Mark Stevens.
   Originally published by Times Books in 2000—E-CIP galley.
   1. Marketing.   I. Title.
   HF5415.S786   2003
   658.8—dc21   2003007947

ISBN 0-609-60983-1

10 9 8 7 6 5 4 3 2 1

First Edition

To the creators of all the cheesy commercials I watched as a kid, which made me bug my mother to buy cereals I detested so that I could win a horse (which would have had to be housed in a one-bedroom apartment in Queens). That was marketing!

CONTENTS

Your marketing sucks.

Read this first

If the moola you spend on marketing isn't growing your business and bringing in more moola in return, then you have marketing that . . . sucks

Welcome to Extreme Marketing

PROBLEM

Knowing what's the best way to achieve your company's overall objectives.

SOLUTION

Extreme Marketing, the process by which you can (a) determine how every marketing dollar can be spent most effectively and (b) receive a positive return on your investment.

BENEFIT

You make more money. You grow your business. You increase its value (which is the true measure of business/financial success) and reap the rewards that come with it.

RULE

1

You will engage in Extreme Marketing, which means every marketing dollar you spend will bring in more than $1 in return.

W hy on earth would I say that "your marketing sucks," much less give a book this title? Because, in fact, the marketing at most companies—big and small— has little, if anything, to do with what is needed to grow the business. Just the other day, I had an experience that, while unusual, is a near-perfect illustration of what I see as a big problem. Three entrepreneurs, each president of his own company, came to my office in suburban New York to hire my company to create a series of ads for them. (My firm does whatever it takes to help a client grow; sometimes that involves creating ads.)

The men have known one another for years, referring business back and forth. That made sense. One sold insurance. Another was an investment advisor, and the third did estate planning.

They had decided to join forces and create one company so that their clients could benefit from one-stop shopping for financial services and experience the benefits of a holistic approach to managing their finances.

The entrepreneurs expected it to be a quick meeting.

They'd pitch some creative ideas. We'd throw out a couple of our own and, voilà, there would be an ad campaign for their merged company.

I think they were shocked that it didn't go that way.

"What are you guys going to call your company?" was my first question once the small talk was out of the way.

"We're not sure yet."

"What's your selling proposition?" I asked.

"We haven't figured it out yet."

"How are you different from the competition?"

Silence.

After that silence dragged on for about fifteen seconds, I jumped in—with a sledgehammer.

"Let me see if I have this right. You want to run a series of ads for a company that doesn't have a name, doesn't know what it's selling or how it's different, and . . . doesn't even exist?"

No joke

This situation, while extreme, is far too typical. It also explains where the title of this book comes from.

Most marketing does suck. And it does because people haven't thought through what they are trying to accomplish before they start spending money on marketing.

They don't engage in Extreme Marketing, which at its

essence means that you need to do everything possible to guarantee that every marketing dollar you spend

a. Is set in a strategic context—that is, you know why you are spending it (for example, advertising "because we have to advertise" is *not* a strategic context)

b. Is based on a plan constructed to make certain that every marketing tactic and tool reinforces every other you are using

c. Brings back more than $1 in return

If you don't employ Extreme Marketing—that is, if your plan doesn't meet the above criteria—then your marketing sucks. And it doesn't matter if we are talking about marketing at a big company or a small one. Size is irrelevant. Your company needs to engage in Extreme Marketing—and most likely it isn't.

Why? For the most part, small companies don't do it because no one at the firm has the expertise. And at big companies, no one has a real vested (my backside is on the line; the money is coming out of my pocket) interest in the effectiveness of the marketing.

I am not exaggerating.

As I write this, it is my favorite time of the year—the period between Thanksgiving and Christmas. Why am I so happy? Well, I will be spending time with family and friends, of course, but another reason is that I know I am about to make a lot of money. Every day for the next couple of weeks, the phone is going to ring, and on the other end of the line is going to be one of my Fortune 500 clients. The conversation is going to go like this:

"Hey, Mark. Listen, I was just going through our marketing budget for this year, and it looks like we're going to have money left over. We are about $XXX,000 under plan. If I don't spend it, senior management is going to cut my budget for next year. Do you think you could do something for us next year, if I sent over the $XXX,000 now?"

As far as I know, not one of my Fortune 500 clients has ever offered to rebate the money back to corporate if he found he had marketing funds left over for the year. They'd rather spend it on anything than risk having their budgets cut for next year.

No wonder their marketing sucks. To so many businesspeople, it's all about spending money—not growing their business.

What we are going to do in the pages ahead

This book will teach you how to become an Extreme Marketer, someone who gets a positive return on her marketing investment. We are going to do that by talking about both strategy and tactics.

By the time we are done talking about strategy, you will be able to make sure that

a. Your marketing efforts are in total alignment with your company's growth/profit/value-building objectives.

b. You are clear about your unique selling proposition. (You can stand for only one primary thing. Otherwise you will confuse your current and potential customers.)

c. You know what it is going to take to reach the broadest possible audience for your product or service.

d. Qualified prospects—including existing customers—will find your offer nearly impossible to resist.

And when it comes to tactics, by the time we are finished you will know why you need to be able to

► Describe what you are selling in a single sentence

► Differentiate what you are selling from the competition in such a powerful way that buying from anyone else will strike a prospect as dumb

► Determine the best prospects to sell to

► Have systems in place to allow you to do that selling efficiently

► Capture leads

► Know exactly how you are going to follow up on those leads

- Cross-sell your products and services to customers/prospects
- Grow your business like a snowball rolling down a hill, steadily gaining speed and mass each day

Extreme Marketing is good business in microcosm. Let's go to work.

I. Why your marketing sucks

Stop throwing thousand-dollar bills out the window and camouflaging spending as marketing

PROBLEM

Your marketing programs are not as successful as you want. Or they are not successful at all (in ways you can measure).

SOLUTION

Scrutinize everything you are (and are not) doing. Put it all under a microscope. Be a skeptical SOB about every dollar you are spending. Keep those programs generating the highest returns. Eliminate everything else, no matter what.

BENEFIT

Your company will grow—profitably.

RULE

Marketing is not about spending money on such things as advertising, direct mail, and P.R. Those are just tools. Marketing is about growing your business—its revenues, profit, and valuation.

If you saw someone open an office window and start tossing out handfuls of thousand-dollar bills, you would have every reason to think that he's nuts. Yet that's what happens in business day in and day out, as company after company wastes millions of dollars on *spending* camouflaged as *marketing*.

These three quick examples are representative. Consider:

- Auto and truck companies spend a fortune sending camera crews to exotic locations to film expensive cars going down twisting, scenic roads. Great imagery. Beautiful direction. Stunning visuals. Now, find me one single human being who bought a car or truck as a result of one of those ads. In fact, find me someone who can tell all those ads apart. Or better yet, someone who can link one of the cars being advertised to a particular scenic road.

- The ad agency your company uses is hot. It just won a Clio, the industry's version of the Oscar, for its last campaign, and the very hip, very cool creative director is showing you the storyboards for this season's big ad blitz for your product. You sign off on the idea, which, when it hits, generates all kinds of buzz in the ad community—but not in the marketplace, where it counts. Your sales don't improve. When management starts asking, "Why are we spending all this money and getting so little to show for it?" you start talking about the value of building "mind share" as a key part of your advertising and marketing strategy. What the hell is "mind share"? The only thing that puts dollars in the bank is *market* share, and Clios don't do that (except for the ad agency that wins them).

- An established, family-owned upscale retailer decides to open a new sales channel by leveraging the power of the Internet. It spends $100,000 to acquire the perfect dot-com name, and it is money well spent. It becomes the first designation that customers think of when they are looking to shop the product category online. But the site is shameful, a disaster. While management was willing to spend $100,000 for the dot-com name, the company spent only $8,000 on the website design—and it shows. The products do not look appealing. It is hard to navigate the site, and worse, you can't find the "hot merchandise" that the company was promoting in its stores and ads. So what appeared to be a powerful sales tool—an industry-leading Web destination—turns out to be the devil in disguise. Instead of spurring sales, it frustrates potential customers.

These three examples are far too typical. Smart people do stupid things all the time when it comes to marketing.

Since the art and science of marketing is not their core expertise, not surprisingly, their marketing is far less effective than they dream it will be.

It's a trap that is easy to fall into. Think of it this way. There is a Christmas-morning sense of excitement when you get your company's new brochure with its pretty pictures or see yourself hawking homemade hickory furniture in a cable-TV ad. In the back of your mind, a little voice says, "We're big-time. We're on television. We have a beautiful brochure. We're *marketers*. Wow!"

But hold it a minute. You know how they say, "Anyone can be a parent. Being a *good* parent is where the tricky part comes in." Well, a similar dynamic occurs with marketing. All you need to market your business is money. You don't need an iota of creativity, smarts, experience, or savvy. No, all you need is a checkbook. And with that checkbook, you can buy ads up the kazoo, public relations that can make Donald Trump look like a recluse, brochures to fill warehouses, websites that would make Steven Spielberg envious.

The problem is that if you are like most companies, all of that spending will result in a negative return on investment. Your marketing will cost you more profits than it brings in.

Why?

Because, in all likelihood, *your marketing sucks.*

Take the *Your Marketing Sucks* diagnostic

Before you get all lathered up and start ranting, "How the hell does *he* know?" ask yourself a few telltale questions.

> Do sales rise every time you advertise?
>
> If so, why don't you advertise every day? In more media?
>
> Have you ever performed a cost-benefit analysis to see if your marketing generates more revenue than it costs to produce?
>
> Do people read your brochure? When was the last time someone commented on it favorably? And more important, when was the last time someone was moved to buy something because of it? Can you track one single sale back to your brochure? Why not?
>
> Do people visit your website? How many? Do these visits lead to sales? Do you have a Web strategy (or just an expensive site with all those pretty animations that make you feel soooooo proud every time you visit your own URL)?

Why most marketing sucks

There are seven key reasons marketing sucks at far too many companies.

1. They don't really know what marketing is,

but in Kafkaesque fashion, they are going to spend money on it. We had a client, a paint company, that had decided it needed a brochure. We told the managers over and over again that wasn't where they should put their money, but they insisted that brochures were a key part of selling paint. Finally, tired of beating our heads against a wall, we designed a beautiful brochure for them that communicated everything the firm did. They printed 10,000 of them. A year later, when I was visiting the company, I wandered into a storage room and found that 9,850 of the brochures were left. I asked why. "These things cost a dollar-fifty apiece," I was told. "You think we're going to send them out willy-nilly?"

2. They go by generalities.

They've heard, for example, that marketing by e-mail doesn't work, so they don't engage in it. Or they accept popular wisdom, like a 1 percent hit rate for direct mail is terrific, writing off 99 percent of their direct-marketing efforts, *blindly accepting that a 99 percent failure rate is a good thing.* The truth is that generalities are worthless, because every situation is different. That's why you have to test what works for you. For example, let's say William Rehnquist, chief justice of the United States, unilaterally decides tomorrow that all speed limits are unconstitutional. He sends out an official e-mail, or a notarized direct-mail letter, that says, "Contact me, and I will send you a card that will automatically get you out of every speeding ticket." Do you think the e-mails would work? Do you think he would get better than a 1 percent hit rate from direct mail? He would make the automatons who think a 1 percent hit rate is great look like the fools they are.

3. They do not employ a swarming offense.

Many of these companies do only one form of marketing—print advertising, for example—and write off people who don't read or who do everything online. You need to hit everyone wherever they turn. Coca-Cola does. It's a great marketer. It's omnipresent. You see its trucks, point-of-sale displays, advertisements—you name it. Everywhere you look, you see Coke's marketing. You can do it, too, on a smaller scale. Lillian August is a five-store upscale furniture chain in Connecticut. Its marketing budget is infinitesimal compared to Coke's. Yet with an annual budget of less than $1 million, the company is everywhere its customers might be: in the Connecticut section of the Sunday *New York Times*. On billboards near its stores. Lillian August gets public-relations placements in the "shelter magazines" like *House Beautiful* and *Architectural Digest*, and it is recognized for its charity work with the American Heart Association.

4. They launch expensive programs and campaigns that are devoid of innovative thinking.

Doing what your competitors do, even if you do it better, is not the way to become a market leader. Remember those gorgeous car ads we talked about? It doesn't matter if your car looks prettier than the competition's as it comes down that long, winding road. Consumers can't tell the ads apart. If you watched TV last night, you saw at least five car ads. Can you name all five? Can you name *one?* Chances are that most of your marketing falls into the same black hole.

5. They ignore readily available research that would allow them to pinpoint ideal prospects.

Databases to reach every conceivable audience are readily available. For example, if you sell annuities, studies show that the most likely buyers of annuities are people who already have at least one, or who have certain demographic (they are sixty-five or older) or psychographic characteristics (they are independent and self-made). Research companies have lists of everyone who owns an annuity and demographic and psychographic lists as well. It's the same for every product or service, and yet the vast majority of marketers don't "profile" the universe of prospects to identify those most likely to buy, even those that glow with neon signs in the various databases. For example, to identify the names of likely buyers of upscale furniture in a given geographical region, we would sort through all of the residents (the universe) by searching for those who live in high-income ZIP codes, are of the thirty-five-to-fifty-five age group, have household incomes of $250,000+, and, to get to the real core prospects, subscribe to three or more home-furnishing magazines. By mixing and matching information from various databases, this profiling can be accomplished. Those with all the right attributes are the ones that "glow." That's where you want to target your marketing first and foremost.

6. Corporate management allows the drivers of the marketing process to remain unaccountable for generating a measurable return on the investment that it takes to produce the marketing programs.

Case in point: When IBM was trying to break into the small-business market, my company created a "mag-a-log" for the giant. It was a magazine-cum-catalog that talked about technology trends—why more small companies were buying servers—and then told you how to buy an IBM server, pointing out what to look for in terms of power, scalability, price, and features. The guy who approved our idea got a raise and a promotion for being innovative. It *was* innovative. It was also a good idea, poorly executed by IBM.

The mag-a-log actually cost IBM money, because it didn't generate enough business to cover its cost. (Why? IBM had no way to sell to consumers directly, and people wouldn't bother to contact an "authorized IBM dealer.") So let's review what happened: The guy who approved an idea without thinking it through got rewarded for costing his company money! Wal-Mart's founder, Sam Walton, would have fired him—not for swinging and missing, but because the guy didn't think! Instead of firing him, IBM gave him a raise.

7. *Managers refuse to admit that the only meaningful return on investment is measured by:*

(a) the recruitment of new customers and/or (b) the sale of additional products to existing customers. Why are they the sole meaningful measures? They are the key factors that lead to increased growth, profitability, and valuation.

You are trying to move product and/or services. Period.

Most businesspeople who should know better (and do know better in every other aspect of their business) equate "creative marketing" (it wins awards) with "effective marketing" (it brings in more money than it costs). Not drawing that distinction is just dumb.

To eliminate this confusion, I have a simple solution: Every company, and every firm they employ, should be forbidden to enter any marketing or advertising contest. No more submissions for Clios. No more "most creative ad by a Midwest agency" competitions. No more *nothing* that has to do with ego as opposed to sales. The reason for that is simple: Ad agencies and the companies that hire them have opposite goals. Those creative directors want to win Clios on your budget—to them, their careers come before your company's growth. So before you hire an agency, you have to forbid it from entering any advertising contest.

The only exception I would make is when the agency is competing for an award that is given for producing the greatest return on investment, and even then I am not sure I would have firms entering those contests—filling out the entry forms takes away from productive work. If someone wanted to give them the award, that would be fine.

Forbes gave my company such an award for an ad we created. (See page 30.) The ad drove an unbelievable amount of traffic to the Cognet website, and that is what it was designed to do. We didn't enter a contest to win it—*Forbes* found us.

Bill Bernbach, one of the guiding lights of the advertising business, once said, *"The best way to get clients is to create good advertising, and I mean advertising that sells."* Amen! And this gospel applies to all of marketing. That is why infomercials, something we will talk about in detail in Chapter 3, are terrific. (And if your first, second, and third reac-

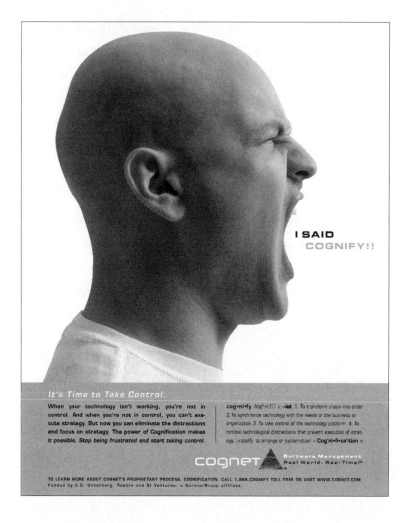

tions are *"We would never do infomercials, because they are so tacky,"* you are probably more interested in how your advertising looks than how it works.)

To be effective, marketing must produce positive arbitrage—that is, it has to generate more dollars than the dollars you invest in it.

Simple? It would appear that way, but in the real world, something gets lost in the translation. Instead of concentrating on the money that good marketing can generate, that Christmas-morning glow ("Look, Ma, we're marketers") replaces the need to demonstrate a strong return on investment.

But when the return on your investment isn't there, there can be no arguing that your marketing sucks. This book tackles the problem head-on. It will help you

- ► Rid your company of spending camouflaged as marketing, and redirect your dollars to programs that deliver strong and measurable financial rewards. (If you get the Christmas glow too, that's fine, but keep the ego-gratification stuff to yourself. We're in pursuit of dollars here.)
- ► Stop overlooking simple but obvious ways of increasing sales and earnings. (For example, you will be amazed to see how easy it is to sell additional products or services to existing clients. We will be talking about that in detail later.)
- ► Use new technologies—or technologies that may be new to you, such as sending "voice messages" to databases of remarkably qualified prospects—to generate more business.

My goal is to help you grow your company, using a proven process that delivers a roundhouse punch into the marketplace. Anything less is a waste of your time and your money.

If you don't have the guts to change the way you've been doing things, open your office window, toss out gobs of thousand-dollar bills, and you'll accomplish the same as you're doing now in much less time.

You are not alone

Of course, if you don't want to change, you can always console yourself with the fact that you are not alone. The problems we have talked about exist across the board.

I have seen it from both sides of the desk. I have worked with Fortune 100 companies (IBM, American Express, John Hancock) as well as start-ups and small companies. They have all had significant flaws.

And I have seen these problems as a consumer.

Case in point: I have been a client of Salomon Smith Barney for more than a decade. It is the firm that manages most of my money. One night, I was struck by a question I couldn't answer: Why, I wondered, did I rarely hear from my Salomon Smith Barney financial consultant?

Other firms contacted me all the time with interesting ideas that I took advantage of, such as a mutual fund that invested in small Asian companies, and a real-estate investment trust. But I almost never heard from Salomon Smith Barney.

The more I thought about this, the more I realized that for years I had received sparse information from the firm. Contact was limited to my account statements, which were distributed with all the flare of a FedEx tracking report. They showed me what I owned, and how much its value had changed since the past statement, but that was it.

It made no sense! Here was a firm rich with talented men and women steeped in investment know-how—from blue-chip stocks to complex derivatives and hedge funds — but a firm that rarely funneled this knowledge to its individual client base, customers like me.

This "smart machine" was never directed to where it could produce a tremendous return for the company: dealing with the clients whose money it already managed. I was already a customer. If SSB had told me that it had a mutual fund that invested in small Asian companies—and it does— I would have gone with SSB, instead of one of its competitors. Trying to sell more to its established customer base would be a simple and extremely effective way to increase revenues and profits.

As I thought about the opportunities SSB was missing, I started to recognize two undeniable facts:

1. The system is dumb. Salomon Smith Barney (like its peers throughout the financial-services industry) invests a fortune in hiring and training superb financial minds but fails to direct their thinking to clients. Everything is

supposed to go through the financial consultants, but if you are like me and don't trade a lot, you have minimal contact with your financial consultant. As a result, clients are deprived of a resource that could help them maximize their portfolios and achieve their financial goals.

2. This idiocy has nothing to do with the firm's knowledge bank. Blessed as it is with an army of investment bankers, financial consultants, certified financial planners, fund managers, and the like, SSB has more than enough resources to help every one of its clients raise the bar on his or her financial performance.

The real failure was in something the financial wizards pay precious little attention to: Extreme Marketing. SSB needed to find a way to direct every bit of its marketing efforts to increasing its revenues.

Moved to action by this epiphany, I phoned Salomon Smith Barney's vice president of marketing to say that our firm should do SSB's marketing. Calling his number—expecting to leave an after-business hours voice mail—I was surprised to hear my prospective client on the other end. That's when I pounced:

"This is Mark Stevens. I would welcome the opportunity to introduce you to MSCO, my marketing firm, and the services we provide."

Marketing vice president: Thanks, but we're already well served. I appreciate the call—

Mark Stevens: Not really.

Marketing vice president: Not really, what?

Mark Stevens: You're not really well served.

Marketing vice president: I think I'm in the best position to judge that.

Mark Stevens: Respectfully, I have to disagree.

Marketing vice president: Look, I don't mean to be rude, but I don't have time to get into a pissing contest. I know you'd like to pitch your firm to me, but there's no opportunity here. So please, if you have nothing else to say, I really have to go.

Mark Stevens: But I do have one more thing to say.

Marketing vice president: Which is?

Mark Stevens: Your marketing sucks.

(LONG SILENCE.)

Marketing vice president: And that very biased view is based on . . .

Mark Stevens: On the fact that I'm a client of the firm—a Salomon Smith Barney client for more than ten years—and in all that time, you've never tried to enrich my experience with the firm. To recommend new investment ideas. To suggest investments in mutual funds. To update me on your fee-based consulting division.

It's as if I don't count. And if it were only
about me, it would probably be just fine for
Salomon Smith Barney. But chances are the
same is true for most of your clients, the millions
of men and women who make you one of the
largest financial-services firms in the world.
The fact is, we are being ignored, overlooked,
and disregarded. It's not because you don't
have the products, services, and skills to meet—
in fact, to exceed—our expectations: It's because
your marketing sucks.

Another long silence followed. Had I overstepped my
bounds? Was he still on the line? Did I have to write off this
prospect for good?

Just when I thought I had in fact gone too far, beautiful
music came over the line.

Marketing vice president: Are you willing to come
in and tell that to our marketing director?

Within days, I was sitting on the twenty-second floor
of Salomon Smith Barney's Manhattan corporate head-
quarters, serving as the unwelcome messenger to an entire
department of marketing executives who wanted to toss
me from the window into oncoming traffic on the streets
below. That was true of everyone except the marketing

vice president, who was enlightened enough to accept corporate criticism, even when it hurt. Smart people can accept criticism, especially if it can help them make more money.

Recognizing that I had identified a glaring weakness in the firm's business model—and that I had an action plan for addressing it efficiently and expeditiously—he hired MSCO on the spot. (I will tell you the results a bit later in the chapter.)

Salomon Smith Barney's myopic marketing was hardly an anomaly. Over the years, I'd discovered a fault line that lay beneath millions of companies large and small around the world. The truth is that in virtually every case, their marketing sucks.

Let's briefly explore a few glaring but all-too-common examples.

• For decades, it seems, Archer Daniels Midland Co. has spent tens of millions of dollars each and every year advertising the company on the Sunday-morning talk shows, positioning itself as "Supermarket to the World." The problem is that ADM is not a supermarket, doesn't own supermarkets, and, even worse, fails to inform viewers of what it really is and what it sells. In typical "your marketing sucks" fashion, it shovels a fortune to the networks to get on the airwaves without explaining its value proposition—and it thinks it is "marketing." The company is in the commodities business, and as far as I can figure, the ads are designed to raise the company's profile so that senators, congresspeople, and White House officials are more receptive when it comes to the firm's lobbying for price supports for things like ethanol, but you'd never know it from those ads.

- Ford Motor Co., much like GM and DaimlerChrysler and most of the import car companies, fails to identify and approach the best prospects for the purchase of a new vehicle. Given today's data-mining technology, Ford is fully capable of isolating the names of GM customers whose leases are about to expire on Chevy Blazers. Once Ford knows who they are, the company's marketers can send those people a letter acknowledging their need to select a new car and offering a gift to those who test-drive a Ford Explorer.

- Upscale retailer Neiman Marcus fails to religiously collect customer e-mail addresses. This one bit of data could enable Neiman's to drive promotional announcements directly into its customers' laptops, offering them first option to purchase new merchandise or to benefit from special sales. Instead, the company focuses on the far more expensive (and often less effective) initiatives of direct mail and advertising.

- CVS, a regional chain of drugstores located in the Northeast, engages in much of its customer contact (with both new and existing customers) through its pharmacy departments. You know how the system works: Customers call in a prescription, and when they stop in to pick it up, they must pass through a maze of aisles brimming with discretionary items from cologne to tooth whitener. At first blush, it looks as if CVS has its marketing act together. The "necessity purchase" (the prescription) drives the store visit, and the retail layout fosters the cross-selling of other goods. But CVS, like many retailers, is guilty of marketing that sucks: It leaves millions of dollars on the table. Why? It fails to engage in a tight integration of all the marketing resources the company has at its disposal. Consider this: Although many customers do purchase the discretionary items that the cross-selling floor plan is designed to encourage, millions more don't. They make a beeline from their car to the pharmacy counter to their car again without buying a single extra item. (Indeed, many CVS stores now have drive-through service so customers never even have to enter the store if they are coming just to either pick up or drop off a prescription.) If 5 million of these in-store visits resulted in incremental sales of $10 each, CVS would rack up an additional $50 million in revenue annually—without spending one additional dollar in marketing. The Extreme Marketing approach, which is always laser-focused on expanding the customer base and increasing sales and profits, would simply require that the staff manning the pharmacy phone lines ask of customers who call in a prescription: "Is there anything we can get for you while your prescription is being filled?" But it wouldn't stop there. If you just ask, "Is there anything else

I can get you?" the customer is likely to say no. So we would tell CVS to word the question this way: "Is there anything we can get for you while your prescription is being filled— do you need shampoo, deodorant, toilet water, toothpaste, or skin lotion? We'll be happy to get anything you need and have it ready for you when you pick up your pre- scription." What a wonderful way to demonstrate excellent customer service. And what a powerful way to drive incre- mental sales. CVS's failure to do so—and thus its failure to do everything possible to generate maximum sales— is a classic case of Lazy Marketing.

What is the solution to Lazy Marketing? Extreme Marketing.

Welcome to Extreme Marketing

There are a lot of wobbly ideas about marketing in today's world, and Extreme Marketing makes you clear-eyed and focused about what needs to be done to be effective. I think of this as "the straight-line test."

Here's how it works. List all of your marketing pro- grams—advertising, public relations, trade shows, direct mail, etc. Then see if you can draw a relatively straight line from the program to a positive return on the money invested and/or an increase in your company's value. If you can't, it is time to substantially improve the program, or dump it. This is Extreme Marketing in its purest form.

My supposition is that you are not now practicing Extreme Marketing. In fact, my guess is that your marketing effort is a lot like my dog Blue.

You'd like Blue. A sweeter, more loyal dog—he's a golden retriever—has never walked on four legs. Sure, he could afford to lose a few pounds, but if you're looking for a warm body to lie at your feet or lick your face, you couldn't pick a better dog.

But while Blue is the perfect pet, he'd be a lousy marketer.

Let's say the UPS deliveryman is a potential customer for Blue. How does he react? Well, you can hear the UPS truck pull onto my street, but even when Blue hears the roar of the engine, he doesn't look up. He doesn't move as the UPS man strides up my front walk. And he doesn't react when the delivery guy reaches the door. It is only after the UPS man rings the bell that Blue goes running to the door, and when he gets there, the deliveryman is in great danger of being licked to death.

I'm guessing that's like your marketing. It's nice. It's gentle. It's pretty. It may even be sweet. But is it making meaningful contact? Is it grabbing hold of prospects and doing everything possible to sell to them? Most important, is it making you any money?

In business, you can't afford to be like Blue and wait until customers ring your doorbell. To stay with our dog analogy, when it comes to customers, you want a bulldog. It will go after the UPS truck the second it hears it—better yet, since the UPS man comes about the same time each day, you want a bulldog that is anticipating his arrival and grabs his leg and does whatever is necessary to take hold of him and make a sale.

If you want to increase your business, you don't want Blue. You want a relentless bulldog.

Extreme Marketing = Extreme Results.

How to think about Extreme Marketing

Extreme Marketing is the antithesis of traditional Lazy (i.e., "it sucks") Marketing. It is based on the following set of guidelines.

1. Marketing is an integrated process—

one in which all of your marketing tactics, such as advertising, telemarketing, and direct mail, should work together to drive sales, whether your company's sales occur at a conference table or at a cash register. Marketing is not "spending money" on ads, websites, brochures, direct mail, or anything else. It is the process of generating incremental sales and profits—and thus building valuation.

2. *You need to identify innovative initiatives that can command the attention of the marketplace*

and, in turn, capture market share. Any restaurant can offer "buy a dinner, get a second at half off" to attract new customers. But a new restaurant in Manhattan had the American Express Platinum Card make the offer. And instead of "buy one, get a deal on the second dinner," the restaurant offered 20 percent off the prospect's bill for the first three months. So not only was the restaurant trading on American Express's credibility, since it had none of its own, it was also giving customers another reason to dine at the new eatery often—they would get 20 percent off each time they did.

3. *Integrate all of the elements of your marketing program*

so that they reinforce each other and drive toward a sale. Examples: Your ad should contain your website address. Your brochures should feature visuals of your ads.

4. *Do not engage in any marketing initiatives that fail to produce a positive return on the money invested.*

If you can't prove that a marketing program is generating more income than it costs you to run it, and you can't correct that, stop the marketing program. (Remember the straight-line test.)

5. Pick the low-hanging fruit.

Every business allows substantial revenues to go by the boards because it is blind to opportunities that are relatively easy to cultivate (e.g., CVS cross-selling). We immediately began working to pick the low-hanging fruit (something we will discuss in detail in Chapter 8) when we started working with Salomon Smith Barney. SSB has a huge advantage over just about every direct marketer: Its established client base is always going to open something labeled "Your monthly statement inside."

Once the customers opened their account statements, we made sure that they would also learn about the firm's latest fund offering; and if there had been a recent news story featuring some of the firm's best investment ideas, it was included as well.

These simple changes made a difference immediately: Orders started to come in.

6. Don't be linear.

People say, "We will run our ads in the newspaper in January, do direct mail in February, and mail the brochures in March." Instead of taking this approach, launch a series of initiatives at once and make a bigger splash. Take an asymmetrical, swarming approach. An upscale retail client was doing plenty of things right when we first started to work with it. But the company was reluctant to do even more at once. For example, we suggested that in addition to all the programs the client was doing, it could send a letter to its house file of twenty thousand names, and it could beef up its website substantially. All of a sudden, the company was engaging in Extreme Marketing, and sales—and more important, earnings—soared.

7. Be persistent, relentless, inventive, counterintuitive, challenging, combative, strategic, and tactical.

Don't accept any marketing maxim unless you have proven that it works for your company. Remember that Sam Walton was told that the dumbest thing he could do would be to build huge stores in small, backwater towns? He heard repeatedly that there wouldn't be enough people to support his stores, and the few people who were there wouldn't have enough money to spend. Walton didn't listen, and today Wal-Mart is the world's retail Goliath, accounting for $1 out of every $7 spent through the nation's retail channel.

In the pages ahead, we are going to provide business owners and corporate managers with a process for identifying the marketing mistakes they are making and the opportunities they are squandering.

Most important, we are going to give you a blueprint for achieving success through real-world-tested Extreme Marketing.

What's ahead: How this book can help you

We are going to tell you why your marketing sucks, but unlike a dilettante professor of business at an Ivy League university who wouldn't know the real world if he fell on it, we aren't going to stop there. We will go to the all-important next step of helping you build an Extreme Marketing blitz.

But before we get there, a few words of warning. Extreme Marketing requires that you question all the rules of marketing you have ever heard, rules such as that you need to spend 6 percent (8 percent, 33 percent) of your revenues on marketing. Questioning conventional wisdom is hard to do. We often accept these "rules" as correct, since we have heard them so many times, but you *have* to question them, because they often turn out to be wrong, or silly, or both.

Let me give you an example. We have all heard the axiom that 90 percent of your body heat leaves through your head. That is just as accepted as the fact that if you are a retailer, you have to advertise. Well, if 90 percent of your body heat leaves through your head, how come you can't put on a hat and go out and play naked in the snow without getting cold?

Think that's silly? Well, so is accepting that you will never get more than a 1 percent response rate on your direct mail. (Remember Chief Justice Rehnquist's "offer" to get you out of all speeding tickers?) Accepting someone else's rules is self-limiting. It tells you—or your agency—that failing 99 percent of the time (as in the case of direct mail) is okay.

You need to question every rule. And the rules that don't pass the Extreme Marketing test—that is, those rules that are not going to lead directly to you making a profitable sale—need to be thrown out the window.

If you discover that those cable ads your company may be running aren't doing one darn thing for your business, yes, you will miss that glow that comes from seeing yourself on TV. But you will get an even bigger glow every time you go to the bank to make the incremental deposits that Extreme Marketing makes possible.

Let's see how you get those bigger deposits.

2. Nothing happens until a sale is made

Any company making sales the last step in the marketing process has its marketing program ass-backwards

PROBLEM

You aren't getting the revenues you expect, even though all your marketing programs are integrated and make sense.

SOLUTION

Get someone who can sell—and he doesn't need to have "salesperson" in his title.

BENEFIT

Soaring sales.

RULE

Most companies make salesmanship the last step in the marketing process. Most companies are wrong: Salesmanship should come first.

Thomas Watson Sr. was one of the extraordinary people in business history. The company he created—IBM—is testimony to his exceptional capabilities as an entrepreneur, visionary, and manager.

Interestingly, when people think of the creation of IBM, and the global behemoth it became, their thoughts turn first to the company's technological prowess. Although technology is certainly important to the IBM story, it was really not the most critical driver of the company's growth under Watson's tenure. The great man himself recognized that when he made the remarkable (for its insight and simplicity) observation—stated in a number of ways to IBMers—that NOTHING HAPPENS UNTIL SOMEONE SELLS SOMETHING.

That statement amplifies a key part of Extreme Marketing. No matter what your company offers, it will never be successful unless it creates and cultivates a powerful sales force able to penetrate the market, interest prospective customers, and close them—that is, get them to buy.

And Watson's credo must be your starting point: **When**

you invest marketing dollars, making the sale is the only acceptable return on investment.

Maybe your sales force won't be the primary driver for you. Maybe it will be direct-response advertising. Or tele-marketing. The specific tactic dosn't matter. The important lesson from Watson's axiom is that it is imperative for every company, large or small, to consider the critical need for achieving the sale at the outset of planning the integrated marketing process.

In other words, you must make certain that your marketing process is designed so that it leads to measurable sales. Unless this occurs, you are destined to waste time and money.

There are countless reasons for why this waste is pervasive through the business world. One of the most prevalent is that the company's marketing is often removed from the sales process. In these situations, the people creating the marketing strategy operate from an altitude of forty thousand feet.

Let me give you a classic example. Many executives in the financial-services industry have received promotions and raises for having one simple insight: You can use accountants as a distribution channel.

The reasoning is simple and, on the surface, makes compelling sense. Most accountants have a great relationship with their clients, and, equally important, they understand the clients' financial status and needs. And so, the reasoning goes, if you provide accountants with a product they can recommend, customers will trust their advice and buy, and everybody is going to make a lot of money.

It sounds like the mother of all marketing insights.

But these financial-services executives all forget one critical thing: Accountants can't sell anything to anyone. For most of them, a telephone is an electric fence. They would never think of picking it up to sell a client or even to ask for business over a perfectly delightful lunch. ("Ask for *business*," the accountant says in horror. "What do you think I am? I am a professional, damn it.") So a seemingly terrific idea turns out to be another form of marketing that sucks, because people don't think it all the way through to the implementation level. Specifically, they don't understand that the key person in the distribution channel—in this case, the accountant—is incapable of making a sale.

Having accountants (try to) sell a product is a classic example of a marketing program designed at forty thousand feet. To overcome this obstacle to success, my company created a CPA marketing channel for one of our clients, Guardian Life. Rather than leaving it to the CPA to make the sale, we created a new way to help make the sale. We started a separate company, Synergy, that paired the certified public accountant with a professional financial-services salesperson who could close on the opportunities that existed in the CPA's client base.

To understand why this approach was so effective, let's put what was going on in perspective.

Lazy Marketing: The case of fifty CPAs

For most of the nineteenth and twentieth centuries, nothing much changed in the accounting profession. Certified public accountants helped keep the books of their clients, filled out tax forms, and periodically offered management advice (usually only when asked for their opinion).

They didn't have to worry about marketing. It basically wasn't allowed under the terms of their professional bylaws. Much like doctors and lawyers, accountants, up to the end of the 1960s, viewed marketing as a crass form of commerce, one that was beneath their dignity. A car dealer might have to advertise, because he was selling a commodity, but an accountant? Never. Their specialized training and expertise placed them far above the "ordinary" producers of products and services.

But then their world changed. Led by aggressive practice builders in their own profession, and propelled by the growing practice of advertising by other professions—most notably lawyers and doctors—accountants slowly began to advertise in the 1970s. Not surprisingly, competition among

CPAs: Is This How You Run Your Accounting Practice?

If it is, you are throwing away significant revenues.

Preparing tax returns may be important to your practice, but there are additional ways to make the numbers add up for you. Expanding your scope of client services to include personal financial planning can build your wealth—and your clients' wealth.

It's an opportunity SYNERGY can help you explore. As the premier nonprofit organization focused on helping CPAs expand into personal financial services, we serve as your partners in client service and in practice building. SYNERGY is guided by a first-class Board of Advisors, including some of the nation's most prominent CPAs and attorneys.

To learn how you can put the power of SYNERGY to work for your practice, contact:
(Local GA Contact)

accounting firms to recruit new clients soon began heating up. While in the past they would simply hope to get new business when and if clients were dissatisfied with their incumbent firms—the old system is often referred to as

CPAs: It's Time To Make The Numbers Work For You.

1040 shouldn't be the only important number in your professional life.

If it is, you are throwing away significant revenues. Preparing tax returns may be important to your practice, but there are additional ways to make the numbers add up for you. Expanding your scope of client services to include personal financial planning can build your wealth—and your clients' wealth.

It's an opportunity SYNERGY can help you explore. As the premier nonprofit organization focused on helping CPAs expand into personal financial services, we serve as your partners in client service and in practice building.

SYNERGY is guided by a first-class Board of Advisors, including some of the nation's most prominent CPAs and attorneys. To learn how you can put the power of SYNERGY to work for your practice, contact: (Local GA Contact)

SYNERGY

"marketing by waiting for the phone to ring"—leading CPA firms aggressively started pursuing new clients.

As the old, passive methods gave way to active pursuit of new business opportunities, accounting firms embraced marketing as a way to compete more effectively and to grow their practices. Quickly, they engaged in a series of tactical maneuvers and tools—brochures, advertising, and public relations—designed to help them succeed in this new environment.

But because the accounting firms never had a sales culture—in fact, they had derided "salesmanship" as unprofessional—virtually all of their marketing was created without the vision of a sale in mind. They figured that all they had to do was tell the world they existed, and that they were good accountants, and their firms would grow. This myopic view doomed their marketing to failure.

Here's a case in point. When my firm, MSCO, relocated its offices to the commuting suburb of Purchase, New York, the company's arrival was duly noted in the official records kept by the county clerk.

Now that they were actively playing the role of *marketers*, CPA firms monitored the records of those firms that had recently moved into the area, in the hopes of finding prospective clients, and they approached the recently relocated firms with the goal of initiating business relationships.

Approximately fifty CPA firms wrote letters to my company. They described their firm's specific capabilities, and each suggested that someone at MSCO contact them to explore the value of being represented by their firm.

While these direct-mail solicitations varied greatly in

their style and substance—some were highly professional in appearance, while others completely ignored the all-important power of first impressions—they all failed to make a sale, or even to get an interview with anyone at my company.

Among the mistakes the accounting firms made:

• Some failed to personalize the letters, simply referring to the recipients as "Mr./Ms. Business Owner."

• Many used mailing labels on the envelopes. You can almost hear the screaming of "JUNK MAIL" in the background as our management looked at the envelopes.

• Virtually all of the firms said the same things about themselves, relying on banal clichés that positioned their organizations as service firms that fawned over their clients and provided "the highest levels of integrity, service, and quality." There is nothing wrong with that. But this is the price of entry. You *expect* an accounting firm to be "dedicated to its clients' interests" and to conduct itself in a "professional" manner. That isn't a competitive advantage—it is a given. If you are compelled to include information like this, it should be at the very end of your marketing material, not the first thing you present to a prospective client.

• Some included brochures that were firm-centric—that is, centered around the accounting firm—as opposed to being client-focused, showing what they could do for our company. For example, they featured drab photos of the firms' partners as a centerpiece of the brochures. This may be fine for the partners' egos, but no one cares what the partners of an accounting firm look like. Far better would have been a list of prominent clients in my industry, or in the Purchase area, but none of the firms included such compelling information in their marketing packages, even though all it would have taken was getting the existing clients' permission.

All these faults were costly, since I was actually a promising prospect. Although we had used the same accountants for fifteen years, I was unhappy with their performance, especially their failure to provide original thinking on business issues.

It was something that kept gnawing at me over time. For example, I have a vacation home that I don't use very much. Instead, I make it available to clients and employees. The accountants knew that. I thought it might be a good idea if I sold the house to the company—at the market price—so that the firm could pay for it with pretax dollars. When I mentioned this to the accountants, they said, "Great idea." To me, it was an idea *they* should have come up with.

Although the level of dissatisfaction with our existing CPA firm was not of epic proportions, I was certainly open to the idea of exploring a relationship with a more proactive firm that would bring original thinking and creative ideas to our business.

Given my level of discontent, you might assume that I would meet with and consider hiring one of the CPA firms vying for my business. But it never happened. As I said, not one single meeting took place.

The reason traces back to Tom Watson's observation that "nothing happens until someone sells something." That was something that all fifty accounting firms failed to understand.

Their direct-mail letters shared a common feature (which you will soon see is a common flaw): They invited our management to contact them to discuss the possibility of working together. This is a perfect example of Lazy ("it sucks") Marketing. It requires the prospect be the catalyst for a sale by picking up the phone, calling a strange firm, and seeking to arrange a meeting. The accountants, presumably hungry for my business, didn't make the call; they were waiting for me to call them.

That is not how it works when successful companies seek to sell their products or services. They recognize, instinctively, that it is wrong to make the prospect do any kind of homework. If you want to do business with someone, it is your responsibility to do everything possible to get in front of the prospect and truly initiate the sales process. **The more you require a client to do, the less likely you are to make a sale.**

Sales happen either in a conference room, at a cash register, or in a home. But thinking that a letter will serve as a magic wand that will turn a prospect into a client is absurd.

For sales to be made on a consistent basis, a company must go through a process that involves a series of steps, all of which are designed to turn a person or a company they do not do business with into a customer or client.

That is a complex and challenging process that requires a full-court press in the form of a series of tightly constructed action steps.

The graphic on page 61—which I think of as the Mission Critical Flowchart—illustrates the components of the sales process and what must be done to emerge victorious.

Let's run through the components one at a time, to show the Extreme Marketing process in action.

1. First you develop a strategy for winning new business based on the value proposition of your products or services.

This is absolutely critical. No marketing is going to work well unless you know what your value proposition is; that is, unless you know the number one reason that people do (or should do) business with you.

Are you the low-cost leader? Best in breed in terms of quality? The most technologically advanced? You need to be able to deliver the proposition in a sentence. For Corham, a

BUSINESS BUILDING PROCESS

Develop Sales Strategy and Reflect In	Meeting	Obstacles	Secure Victory
• Public relations	• Restate strategy message, capabilities	• Politics	• Find solutions and overcome obstacles
• Advertising	• Client falls in love	• Pricing	
• Websites		• Competition	
• Direct mail			
• Telesales			
• Networking			
• Referrals			
• Database/ Drip			
• E-mails			

home-furnishing store that sells a wide variety of merchandise—accent pieces such as pictures, end tables, vases, silk flowers, and dozens of other products that can be taken off the sales floor and loaded directly into a customer's SUV—Extreme Marketers developed the value proposition "Drive Your Dream House Home." The message: This was *the* place to go to pick the perfect item to complement your home, and you could have that item in your home that same day.

Whatever distinguishes your product or service must be the feature that is used to attract prospective clients and customers. It must be your central message, the one you repeat time after time so that people know exactly what

you stand for, why you are different, why they can't live
without you.

In our CPA example, the value proposition could have
been something like "We are small-business experts who
know how to maximize the value of entrepreneurial com-

panies (so that the owner can become richer), and we just happen to be (terrific) accountants." That is far more effective than the common (implicit) refrain of "We are accountants who happen to know something about business."

Remember, lead with your strongest selling point and stay focused on it. Resist the temptation to provide the same boilerplate everyone else does ("We have the friendliest people and the lowest prices in town") or clutter your message with secondary benefits that you offer. All of that just dilutes the power of your unique qualities. Less *is* more.

2. Communicate the value proposition every way you can.

Once the value proposition is developed, you then create messages that are sent to the prospective customer/clients through direct mail, e-mail, advertising, or public relations—or, most powerfully, through a combination of these components unleashed simultaneously. You want to seem omnipresent in the minds of your prospects. Of course, you can send your messages sequentially, but you will have a far greater impact if everywhere a prospective customer looks he sees your message.

3. The customer must fall in love.

Once the sales opportunity materializes—and that opportunity can be an informal one on a busy retail floor or a formal one held in the conference room—one critical thing must happen: The prospect must *fall in love* with the pursuing company and/or its products and services.

People buy not when they *like* something or think it is satisfactory but when they are overwhelmed by its capabilities and believe they cannot, or do not want to, live without it. Trying to accomplish anything less than that is a prescription for slow growth at best and, more likely, the failure to operate as a going concern over time.

If you have been successful enough to arrange the meeting, and to make the prospect *fall in love*, there is still work to be done. In the vast majority of cases, even after a prospect believes that he wants to purchase your product or service, something gets in the way before the actual sale is consummated. This can be as predictable as prospective buyer's remorse, political conflict inside the company (this most frequently occurs in the case of a business-to-business sale) that questions the need for the product or service, or a lowball price by a competitor asked to bid at the eleventh hour.

Companies that come through this critical part of the sales cycle reach back to the prospect to determine how things are going and if an agreement can be consummated. In this process, they may discover that significant issues are forming that may preclude a sale. Having this knowledge is of great importance, because it enables the pursuing company to take the action it needs to make the sale in spite of whatever barriers have risen since the initial meeting.

For example, to overcome those barriers the company can:

- ► Lower its price
- ► Offer additional services to compensate for its higher pricing
- ► Provide an extended warranty
- ► Offer a trial period that enables the prospect to buy with a clearly defined exit clause in case it is unhappy with the company's products and services

In many cases, this last-minute horse-trading makes the difference between companies that walk away empty-handed and those that bag the sale and begin the customer/client relationship.

Let's see how all of this works in the real world, in the case of a professional-services firm that successfully recruits new clients by taking the steps that the fifty CPA firms failed to.

What the accountants should have done

My colleagues and I work with a leading law firm to attack a problem common to virtually every professional-services firm: The vast majority of the partners and associates may be excellent technicians, but they are unwilling or incapable of generating client relationships and the fees associated with them.

Practice building, each partner will freely tell you, is not his forte. Besides, he didn't become a lawyer (accountant/doctor/architect/engineer) to *sell*. If he wanted to be a salesman, he would have gone into sales. And in fact, as we have seen, there is an inherent cultural bias against selling throughout professional-services firms. And so the *professionals* prefer to leave it to others in the firm.

The problem with this is that it puts the burden of generating revenues and firm growth in the hands of a few people. The bigger the practice becomes, the more rain the few business developers have to make in order to achieve consistent growth.

Over the years, professional firms have sought to address this difficulty by providing their partners with "sales training," whereby they are "taught" to develop skills that will help them be more effective in turning prospects into clients. The problem is that this tactic runs counter to another basic tenet of Extreme Marketing:

You cannot turn a nonsalesperson into a salesperson, and you cannot stop a salesperson from selling.

Invariably, service professionals—with the exception of the people who founded the company—are not salespeople. Entrepreneurs by definition are salespeople, but frequently the people they employ are not. Therefore, the time, talent, and money spent on trying to magically turn those professionals unable to initiate or expand client relationships into sales stars through store-bought salesmanship is wasted.

There is no secret formula, no potion you can employ that will turn an individual incapable of "selling" into a rainmaker.

The fact is that salespeople bring in business. They bring home the check. That is what sales is about. It is not the ability to put on a pleasant presentation or have a good meeting. Salespeople aren't afraid to make cold calls, they are eager to ask for the sale, they have a passion for what they do, they don't fear rejection, and they are bulldogs. (They aren't like my dog Blue.) They won't stop until they get the business. You either have those traits or you don't.

If you don't, does that mean Extreme Marketing is wasted on you? **Absolutely not. It just means you need real salespeople in your marketing mix to close the deal.**

The Lazy Marketing approach is to deny this undeniable fact and

a. Continue to hope for this magic
b. Accept the fact that only a few of the individuals in the firm will produce practice-building results

The Extreme Marketing methodology, as applied at the law firm, goes about solving this problem differently.

Instead of seeking to achieve what is virtually impossible

by pressuring, cajoling, and pleading with non–business generators to produce client relationships, Extreme Marketers engage in a process that leaves the professional out of the process of landing new clients, or enhancing relationships with existing clients, until the point that the professional feels comfortable taking over the reins.

It works this way:

1. In consultation with the client, we identify a partner's, or group of partners', professional expertise and crystallize it into a value proposition that will be of compelling interest to a significant percentage of the prospect community.

2. We create messages designed to communicate that value proposition to the prospects in e-mails, snail mail, and telesales.

3. We engage in media relations—press interviews and op-ed pieces—to support this effort.

(Each of these pieces can work alone, but you get a truly synergistic effect if you do all three. As we mentioned earlier, you want a customer—or prospective client—to see you everywhere he looks.)

This one-two-three punch is unleashed as follows:

The prospect is sent an e-mail capturing the essence of the professionals' service and how it can be of immediate value to him.

An e-mail? Won't people dismiss that immediately as spam?

The answer is no, providing you give the e-mail subject line serious thought. "Polo cashmere 50 percent off" is not treated as spam when Ralph Lauren sends it out shortly after Thanksgiving, providing a wonderful gift idea just as the Christmas buying season is about to kick into high gear.

It is your job as the marketer to make sure the message isn't seen as spam. For example, the CEO might receive an e-mail from my firm saying, "Does your marketing suck?" and an accounting firm might send out an e-mail message with the header "Are you risking an SEC investigation?" to promote the firm's ability to make sure a company is in compliance with the reporting regulations that were introduced following the 2002 ethical meltdown on Wall Street.

On the same day that the e-mail is sent, a telesales call is made to the prospect, reinforcing this message. Although the message often finds itself in the prospect's voice mail, this is fine, since it enables the telesales person to actually get the word across briefly and succinctly. The message: "One of our firm's senior people would like to give you an overview on potential legal problems your organization faces—we call these presentations Executive Briefings—and what can be done about them."

A day or so later, the prospect receives a snail-mail message, further reinforcing the professionals' services and inviting him or her to an Executive Briefing, which can be held in the prospect's office, to discuss it further. This is the best role for the marketer: setting up appointments so that the practitioner can get in front of the client.

A week later, prospects who have not yet responded to the one-two-three punch are called again, with the goal of seeking a teleconference or an in-person meeting to further explain and present the concept the firm is seeking to sell.

If the messages are carefully constructed, and the firm is persistent, its actions will result in a series of Executive Briefings, in which the partner goes out to the potential client's office and talks about a problem or opportunity the client faces and what can be done to address it.

Executive Briefings are a way to put a professional—who is armed with talking points that stress his firm's capabilities—in front of an interested prospect.

Those individuals who have not yet responded are placed in a database for ongoing communications.

The power of this approach is that it frees partners suffering from sales fright from having to engage in any form of "selling" and enables them to simply "educate" prospects who have clearly demonstrated a desire to learn about the firm's professional-services capabilities in general, and their own particular expertise.

This change in perception from "selling" to "educating" is a dramatic shift that makes all the difference in the world to a professional who feels that it is either too aggressive or somehow improper to be reaching out to prospects. Professionals who hate the idea of selling love the idea of explaining what they do during an Executive Briefing. They view it as solving problems that a client presents, and not what it actually is: a sales call.

In essence, we invert the model and place the prospect (at least in the professionals' eyes) in the position of seeking the meeting and initiating the relationship.

In the law firm example, the Extreme Marketing process focused on two lawyers, one specializing in white-collar crime and the other in employee-theft cases. Although both are extremely talented attorneys, they needed help in generating additional client engagements.

To make this happen, we implemented the three-step process. For both attorneys:

1. We shaped their areas of expertise into service offerings that would prove to be valuable to businesses in the community. In other words, we created a value proposition for each of them.

2. Then we fashioned this into direct-mail letters designed to make the recipients recognize that it would be in their best interest to meet with the attorneys.

3. We helped them write op-ed pieces and arranged press interviews.

A few days after the direct-mail letters were sent, tele-sales calls were made to the prospects.

Again, the idea wasn't to sell anything over the phone. It was simply to set up appointments to enable the attorneys to educate the prospects on the risks and opportunities their firms faced and, thus, to build business for the law firm by delivering additional services (that could help prospects minimize their risks and capitalize on opportunities).

The results were significant. Of one hundred prospects approached in one of the white-collar crime direct-mail/ telesales programs, seventeen agreed to an appointment.

To properly equip the lawyers for the meetings, we helped them create an agenda that would make sure they answered all the questions a prospect might have about the subject at hand. The presentations were tailored for each potential client's specific interest. The agenda also included talking points so that the lawyers could explain how the clients could help them.

The flowchart on pages 74–75—internally, we refer to it as the Marketing Systems Integrator—explains how this came about.

As we said, concurrent with the direct-mail/telesales campaign, we launched a public-relations initiative, providing widespread recognition of the law firm's expertise. This helped to create awareness and thus soften the market for the letters that would be arriving at prospects' offices.

For our clients, we also create powerful ad campaigns designed to provide air cover for the overall marketing campaign. Case in point: Unlike traditional advertising for professionals—which stress the usual buzzwords ("no one will fight harder for you") and usual images (scales of justice)—we utilize ads like the one below created for our client, the prominent New Jersey law firm of Stark & Stark, to make a strong and memorable impression.

Blindsided

You didn't see it coming. A legal issue that could take tremendous time and money – and throw your business off track. At Stark & Stark, we understand. Because we know business and we know law, and we make the law work for you and your business. You get premier quality legal counsel practiced by attorneys with real-world business savvy – and a proven focus on results. All of which adds up to the kind of advice, insight, and performance you can only get at the new breed of law firm – Stark & Stark. To find out how we can help you get what you want out of your business, make a no-obligation appointment to talk to us and learn about our customized Business Assessment consultations. Contact Lewis Pepperman, Esq., at 1-866-4BIZLAW, or via email at lpepperman@stark-stark.com. We invite you to visit us on the web at www.stark-stark.com.

STARK&STARK
BUSINESS LAW

993 LENOX DRIVE LAWRENCEVILLE, NEW JERSEY 08648   ©2002 STARK & STARK, A PROFESSIONAL CORPORATION

INDIVIDUAL ATTORNEY MARKETING

Hold initial meeting with selected attorney to discuss areas of expertise, marketing focus, primary and secondary target markets, etc.

↓

Develop compelling direct-mail letter indicating value proposition to prospect.

↓

Attorney receives individual and group training on how to work with prospects.

↓

Purchase highly targeted mailing lists.

↓

Mail letters with business-reply cards, which prompt recipients to schedule a meeting or request more information.

↓

Follow up with phone call to schedule meetings:
• In-house for mailing under 250
• Outsourced for mailings over 250

↓

Attorney meets with prospect, armed with:
• Knowledge about the prospect from preparatory research
• "Product" offerings
• An educational approach based on the value proposition

↓

Enter customized prospect information in a database.

↓

Follow up with all prospects, depending on level of interest.

↓

Continue to follow up with all prospects with e-newsletters, update letters, phone calls.

Firm P.R.

Focus on niche practices and position firm as
the leader in the field.

Individual Attorney P.R.

Develop appropriate list of media (dailies, business publications,
broadcasts, and relevant trade press).

Write pitch letters/press releases.

Conduct concentrated P.R. outreach to obtain
media coverage and speaking opportunities.

Utilize P.R. hits—use tear sheets as credibility builders
in direct mail.

First, address the reason the prospect wanted to meet.

Next, attempt to cross-sell.

An immediate letter and phone call detailing a specific
product offering.

An immediate letter and phone call cross-selling the firm's services.

A follow-up phone call two months later.

Now, let's take another look at the critical issue of selling, moving beyond the world of professional services.

We have already talked about the fact that you can't turn a nonsalesperson into a salesperson. But when you dig a little deeper, you find something that is even more depressing, if you are a senior manager or entrepreneur.

The problem can be reduced to this: "Ninety-nine percent of the world's salespeople aren't."

What does this mean? Simply that the vast majority of people posing as salespeople fall into one of the following two camps:

- They have tried other jobs and failed at them, so rather than remaining on the unemployment lines, they are taking a fling at selling. That is certainly not a background that is going to inspire confidence.

- They actually want to be salespeople and may like the idea of selling. After all, they have always been told that they are sociable and outgoing and assume this makes them natural-born salespeople. But although they may be charming, they can't make the sale. The fact is that there is an enormous gulf between a *schmoozer* and a *closer*. The ability to get along famously, and even conduct an amiable sales meeting, does not a salesperson make. The only way a salesperson can be judged is on the ability to actually write new business. And it is on this acid test that most "salespeople" fail miserably.

The problem is of epic proportions and exists everywhere, even in so-called sales-driven organizations, such as life-insurance companies.

Given that no one wakes up in the morning dreaming of buying life insurance and that, for most of us, the purchase of a policy is a joyless process that we would prefer to defer indefinitely, it takes an exceptional salesperson to convince someone to write a check to buy an insurance policy.

The problem is that at any given time, most people who call themselves life-insurance salespeople really cannot sell. The proof is in the numbers: Even those life-insurance companies with the most effective screening, recruiting, and training methodologies for salespeople still encounter turnover rates of more than 75 percent over a given three-year period.

Think about that for a moment: The *best* life-insurance companies—corporations steeped in sales cultures, often for a century or more—lose 75 percent of their salespeople every three years. The reason is that these people were never really salesmen or -women.

If you track the history of the people who wash out, you can see why that is the case. We will discuss a typical case in a second, but first a word of warning.

This is not a sales book. This is a book about how to build your business. And if you want to build your business, you need to recognize that certain people can't sell it—and that is true, even if they have the word "sales" (person,

manager, whatever) in their title. If you have people like that—and I am betting that you do—you must fire them. It is the right thing to do for them—they need to know that they should find another source of work that is right for them. And it is the right move for your business.

It is unpleasant. But it must be done.

The following situation will explain why.

Meet John Doe, insurance agent

Here's the typical scenario: A life-insurance agent joins the company with a great deal of hope that he can actually sell policies. Think of this as *hope springs eternal.*

In this case, it means the person who lands a job as a salesman believes he can sell even if he has had no significant experience in doing so.

Equally important, managers are so hungry for people—after all, 75 percent of their sales force leaves every three years—to move the product that they also engage in copious amounts of hope, believing time after time that they have found the right person, even when all of the vital signs indicate that the person can't sell anything to anyone. They remain hopeful because they are convinced that the company's sales-training programs can turn anyone into the world's best salesperson.

So the hopeful sales manager welcomes the equally hopeful recruit to the company, and the brand-new salesman promptly does the following:

1. Takes what insurance he has on himself or his immediate family and replaces it with a policy from the company that has hired him. So in effect he has made a sale, and hope is rewarded: "Hey, this guy can sell." (Yes, the sales manager knows what is going on, but to him it is a sign of initiative. His new salesman is "gaining traction.")

2. Approaches members of his extended family and—begging for a chance to begin a new career successfully or resuscitate a failed one—pleads with them to buy the adult version of Girl Scout cookies. So he finds some relatives willing to do him a favor, and he makes a sale. The result: Hope is rewarded again ("This guy is building momentum as a salesperson").

3. Approaches friends and engages in the same diplomatic arm-twisting, offering not so much the life-insurance product as the opportunity to demonstrate loyalty to a pal in need. So he makes a sale. The bottom line: Once again hope is rewarded, and the feeling grows that "this guy is a salesperson."

But at this point, just when everyone is happily deceiving himself or herself, the new "salesperson" runs out of clay pigeons. Having made sales to himself, his friends, and his family members, he has to venture out into the real world. That is when the "hope springs eternal" syndrome backfires, and the reality sets in that Joe Salesman is really a schmoozer, at best, who is destined to be among the 75 percent or more who will not make it with the company.

But there is another minichapter in this story that actually compounds the problem and delays the pain. The company—even though it has seen this scenario thousands of times—deceives itself again by believing that all this nonsalesman needs to become a salesman is a mentor or a coach or a training program. Why? Because in rare instances it actually works.

So the novice is paired with a successful closer to serve as his mentor and/or is placed in a training program designed (hope springs eternal) to take him from promising person to star closer. When you look beneath the surface, what this really means is that the company wastes

• The time of the successful producer by forcing him to move through the frustrating processes of trying to turn a nonsalesman into a salesman. Yes, it may work 5 percent of the time—as the successful producer finds selling skills that were laying dormant within the new salesperson—but that means 95 percent of time it won't.

- Managerial time and attention trying to find a way to make the nonsalesman into a salesman.

- Money on training programs that rarely accomplish their goal.

Why do so many big companies pursue these dumb, time- and money-squandering courses of action? There are several reasons. The company

a. Is optimistic.
b. Finds it is easier to do nothing than to actually take action (like firing the incompetent salesman).
c. Is just demonstrating something I believe with all my heart: Big companies can afford to lose money. And so they will put up with the ineptitude far longer than closely held entrepreneurial companies. (That's because the incompetent salesman would be taking money out of the mouths of the owner/ entrepreneur and his family and would be fired without a second thought.) Big companies allow incompetent people to stay on their payrolls far too long,

either out of a misguided sense of trying to protect them—it would be better for all concerned if someone who is not suited to a job is told as soon as this becomes clear—or because of inertia.

As a result of A + B + C, big companies fail to accomplish what they set out to do—create a dynamic sales force —because of what I have described as a fundamental truth: You can't turn a nonsalesperson into a salesperson and you cannot stop a salesperson from selling.

The second part of that statement is as important as the first. Let's look at them together, in the case of a real-world example that will let us see once again how important the process of selling is to Extreme Marketing, and why Lazy Marketing fails miserably to accomplish business goals and to achieve a substantial return on investment.

Lazy Marketing slams profits

When an East Coast–based real-estate company decided to diversify its holdings from office buildings, strip malls, and apartment houses into senior assisted-living residences, management acquired a network of properties throughout the nation. The business plan was sound and offered substantial promise.

Given the dynamics in the senior assisted-living marketplace at the turn of the new millennium, it was possible to buy grandly constructed properties at deeply discounted vulture-investor prices. The market had become glutted, and the majority of assisted-living facilities were losing money due to low occupancy rates; their owners were looking to get out at just about any price.

The business plan was simple (on paper): Buy existing assisted-living facilities at depressed prices, pump up the occupancy levels through heavy marketing, and then resell the properties at substantial profits.

The key to making this work, of course, was to deal effectively with the occupancy issue. Only if the revenue streams associated with the properties increased substantially could the "vulture investors" reap the rewards they had in mind at the outset.

Based on this goal, the company engaged in an aggressive marketing campaign to fill the buildings.

But the campaign was flawed from the start. In classic Lazy ("it sucked") Marketing fashion, management committed several inexcusable blunders. For one thing, the sales personnel hired on-site to sell the properties were schmoozers, incapable of closing prospects. Although they could give cordial and informed tours of the senior living communities, and were decent, hardworking people, they could not

a. Get the prospect to sign a lease

b. Get the all-important check.

The end result of placing the wrong people in the sales role? Occupancy rates failed to increase. In fact, the rate was falling, since a certain number of residents died each year. (These were, after all, senior citizens.) The failure to hire the right salespeople made a mockery of the vulture investors' business model. This is proof positive that Lazy Marketing slams profits, diminishes equity values, and in many cases leads to bankruptcies.

Spurred by the fear of disaster, the new owners quickly activated Extreme Marketing: They implemented a series of critical steps to reverse the flawed situation and swiftly generate a significantly higher volume of prospects and corresponding number of sales.

The biggest move was to dismiss most of the sales staff. Good-bye. *Adios.* Better luck elsewhere. Although this may seem to be a drastic step, analyses of existing personnel indicated that they were incapable of closing sales at a sufficient rate. To replace them, the Extreme Marketers identified the most successful senior living communities in the area and recruited their sales personnel to take over at the company's properties. This provided for immediate transition from schmoozers to closers—or, to use my canine analogy again, they replaced golden retrievers with bulldogs—with the added benefit of bringing in salespeople with intimate knowledge of the marketplace. In short order, occupancy levels climbed dramatically.

This demonstrates clearly the power of salesmanship and the results a business can achieve when it transitions from Lazy Marketing to Extreme Marketing.

In this case, the experienced group of real-estate pros bought the senior living communities based on the premise that by installing superior management and implementing more effective marketing, they could reverse the financial performance of the properties and, ultimately, their market value, thus making this vulture investment highly profitable. But given their lack of marketing prowess, they convinced themselves they were doing everything they could to fill their properties, when in fact a huge gap remained between the initiatives in place and those that could be implemented to raise occupancy and thus the earnings and value of the properties.

This underscores another critical issue: In many businesses, longevity is automatically deemed to equate with excellence. If someone has been with the company for a long time, it is assumed that she is doing a terrific job.

But Extreme Marketers recognize that **longevity is far less important than management's willingness to repeatedly dismiss mediocre performers in order to raise the bar on the company's revenues and profitability.**

No one can deny that building a great team infused with powerful esprit de corps is a worthy goal and a commendable managerial feat, but longevity for the sake of longevity is more likely to lead a business to a slow death than to power it to the top of its industry.

Precisely because the sale is the monomaniacal focus of the Extreme Marketing process, you need to make sure you have closers in place wherever marketing drives prospects near your product or service.

Anything less is a prescription for disaster.

3. Start with a blank page

To hell with what your competitors are doing ... rethink everything and start from scratch

PROBLEM

Your marketing isn't breaking through because it basically looks like everyone else's.

SOLUTION

Ignore the competition. Rethink everything. Start from scratch.

BENEFIT

You will end up with a unique selling proposition that will make you stand out.

RULE

You will never jump ahead of the pack if you accept the conventional wisdom. Healthy skepticism is a good thing. Question every single thing you have heard about the "right way" to market.

See if this sounds familiar:

HealthTech,* a New Jersey–based technology firm specializing in the design and installation of diagnostic equipment used in hospitals, decided it was going to spread the word throughout the health-care industry about its capabilities. Step 1? Management decided to create a top-of-the-line brochure, providing a comprehensive review of its product line.

The company's brochure task force began by spreading the competitors' brochures on the office conference table and indulging in the self-satisfying process of picking them apart. You'll recognize the barbs:

"Too drab."

"Too techie."

"Too much text."

"Too little text."

"Ugly images."

"Not enough images."

---

*A fictional name for a real company.

"No people pictures—too cold."

"Too many people shots. Customers want to see technology, not feel-good people shots."

Then comes the confident proclamation: "We can do so much better!"

Although this may appear to be an effective call to arms that will help conquer the competition, in effect it tends to be a counterproductive exercise.

While the HealthTech team agreed they could outdo the competition's brochures, they failed to recognize that something had changed while they sat around the conference table picking apart the competition. Their mission had shifted from the legitimate business goal of creating a powerful brochure designed to drive sales, to the egocentric exercise of beating what the competition had produced.

In effect, the focus shifted from the battlefield to bragging rights.

You need to control the agenda

Starting any aspect of your marketing process by looking at what your competition is doing is a bad idea. It forcefits your creative process into a locked box and discourages the development of truly innovative and powerful strategies and tactics that can:

1. Create demand
2. Command attention
3. Build brands
4. Drive consumer behavior
5. Change purchase patterns
6. Gobble up market share
7. Increase revenues and profitability

Here's why: When you start the marketing process by studying the competition, you are (intentionally or not) establishing their work (mediocre as it may be) as a benchmark. And (intentionally or not) you are more likely to imitate it than if you start with a blank page.

Intriguingly, this is something that Albert Einstein—someone who didn't care a whit about marketing—understood perfectly. As he was fond of saying, "I am enough of an artist to draw freely upon my imagination. Imagination is more important than knowledge. Knowledge is limited. Imagination encircles the world."

Like a child engaging in cartoon fantasies, Einstein would allow his mind to wander freely, beginning with dreamlike scenarios of "the impossible, the implausible, and the phantasmagoric" ("Suppose gravity didn't exist"), and then he worked backward from these "what ifs" to "what could be."

This "thinking outside the box" liberated Einstein, freeing his mind of all scientific restraints. Instead of sitting down with Newton's laws and looking for gaps he could fill (the scientific equivalent of checking out the competition's brochures), Einstein dreamed of time, space, and movement in new ways.

Interestingly, many of the most successful marketers have used free-form imagination to achieve extraordinary results. Beginning outside the proverbial box—even by going so far out as to engage in fantasy—leads to a much greater likelihood of winding up in fresh and original territory.

You can see the converse with HealthTech's approach. Because the competition's brochures were established as the benchmark, it placed an artificial ceiling on the creative process by prompting the team to begin with the goal of beating something clearly viewed as weak—and then claiming victory once they achieved it.

Most marketing starts this way—and it is no wonder most marketing sucks.

So we say: Ignore the competition. Start with a blank piece of paper or computer screen.

Easy to say, hard to do.

Why is it so hard?

There are a number of reasons. But let's touch on just two. People start with preconceived notions: "We *have* to do our brochure (marketing/P.R./book/whatever) this way. It's the way that everyone else does it." (Remember all those look-alike car ads we talked about earlier? Or how about all those financial/retirement-planning commercials that pan in on a couple in their sixties walking hand in hand on a beach? Do you remember the names of any of the companies that spent millions to present that image?)

Then there's the phobia of confusing customers because you are too creative. If the team comes up with something that has never been done before, will customers "get it"? Will they like it? Invariably, instead of doing something new, the people posing these questions decide to play it safe, figuring it is less of a risk.

But that is just wrong, wrong, wrong! Instead of worrying about what the competition is doing, or whether you will look dumb, you need to consider everything you can to reach the hearts and minds of the customers. The idea is to move outside of existing paradigms and to unleash maximum creativity and original thinking to form the basis of your marketing programs.

When Extreme Marketers were assigned to put a relatively small consulting firm, Crimson Technologies, on the map, the knee-jerk response was to focus on words and images that would reflect the firm's technology prowess. But in the midst of the first brainstorming session, we scotched that idea, recognizing that if we went that route, you wouldn't be able to tell the firm apart from all the other technology-consulting firms out there.

Instead, we developed a positioning based on the theme "Destination Unlimited." Rather than focusing on the tech-

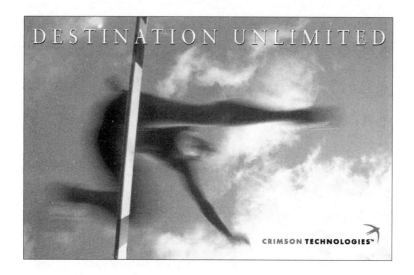

DESTINATION UNLIMITED

CRIMSON **TECHNOLOGIES**™

nology itself, we concentrated on what firms could do with their technology (with Crimson's help). Technology companies all market themselves in virtually the same way: "We are experts at high tech, blah, blah, blah." But most businesspeople don't want to buy technology—they want to invest in tools that will grow their companies. So we established a value proposition for Crimson based on what business technology accomplishes. Thus the tag line "Destination Unlimited," meaning that with the right technology you can take your business in any direction and to unlimited heights. The imagery reinforces this. There are no servers, wiring, network technicians—the entire presentation is that of a company that understands the real power of tech and uses it to build companies. (When you have a minute, take a look at Crimson's website—

www.crimsontechnologies.com—for specifics on how this message is delivered.)

Earning your infomercial M.B.A.

To see unfettered marketing in its purest form, take a look at something you have probably never spent much time pondering: infomercials. Who would have ever thought that you could do a thirty-minute or sixty-minute television program whose sole purpose was to sell something? This is one of the greatest let's-see-what-happens-when-we-think-outside-the-box examples of all time.

What is it that makers of infomercials do, and how do they do it?

Let's put this work in context: You're an intelligent person. One night, you can't sleep, so you turn on the television to help you pass the time. Sure enough, there is an infomercial on the air, with a sleazy guy selling a crazy bodybuilding gadget that intellectually you know will not/cannot work nearly as well as the wonder it is portrayed to be on the tube. You're too smart to fall for that miracle widget.

Or are you? If you are honest enough to admit it, you know you start to fall prey to the infomercial and actually desire the gizmo and to let its magic powers make you thinner/sexier/happier/richer.

Why does this transformation from the *intelligent skeptic* to the *intelligent victim* of infomercial marketing occur? How do these marketers convince you to engage in a willing suspension of disbelief and make you want to reach for your credit card at 3:16 A.M. to buy a real-estate training program that proposes to make you—in three short months—so filthy rich that you will spend the rest of your days sipping piña coladas on a beach while looking down your nose at the working stiffs you used to call your peers?

Here, too, the answer is really simple: If you look closely at infomercials, not necessarily as a consumer but as a businessperson/marketer, you will see that they employ a number of powerful devices that can and should be used in virtually every marketing campaign. For example:

► Give your product a cool and compelling name. Labels like Tummy Cruncher and Money Mentor and Fat Destroyer say, in cryptic but clear fashion, what the product claims to do and reinforce the fact that with all consumers hope springs eternal. Fat people want to get thin, ugly people want to be beautiful, dumb people want to be smart, shy people want to be friendly, old people want to be young, poor people want to be rich, and everyone can and does at one time or another engage in a fantasy that this transformation can be achieved on the strength of a one-a-day pill or an audiotape recorded in a basement in Columbus, Ohio. Hope does spring eternal, and products and service names that reinforce this hope win.

► Remember that a picture is worth a thousand words. Infomercials show how the product works, using the time-honored and still powerfully effective before-and-after approach. In many cases, the main reason you want to reach for your credit card in the middle of the night is because the masters of marketing, infomercial-style, show you in living color how a fat guy got thin, a dirty shirt got clean, a poor girl got rich, and a guy who once had no appeal to women suddenly became a babe magnet. By showing you what appears to be dramatic change, the infomercial makers allow your mind to run wild, saying, most importantly, *that can be me, too.*

► Provide the appearance of exceptional value. The most effective infomercials start with an attractive price for a given product and then—in the course of the commercial—add a series of elements to the offering under the umbrella of the original price. In this context, viewers fail to assess the value of the original price—in fact, they accept it as fair on face value—and then consider the add-ons ("I'll throw in this; I will double the size of that") as freebies that are in many cases too good to pass up. Traditional marketing often says, "Our price is twenty-five dollars. Take it or leave it." Winning infomercial advertising goes ten steps further. It begins by saying: "Our price is twenty-five dollars. But you don't have to accept this as the final offer. Watch as we add bells and whistles to the offering at no additional price. In the end, you wind up with fifty dollars' worth of products for twenty-five dollars [or so you think]. Now, isn't that too good to pass up?"

► **Expose the viewer to testimonials.** Forget about traditional marketing and the complacency associated with it. Case in point is the use of weak cliché testimonials/credentials such as the *Good Housekeeping* Seal of Approval. Does anyone know what this means anymore?

The infomercial makers know full well the power of a compelling testimonial. So they expose viewers to an onslaught of living, breathing, satisfied customers who have used their product and swear by it on a stack of Bibles. If you're an intelligent viewer approaching the infomercial with a healthy dose of skepticism, your defenses begin to melt away as you are exposed to the fourth, fifth, seventh, tenth person who thanks heaven (and the product at hand) for making them rich/thin/beautiful/ageless/smart.

And the beauty of it is that the testimonials are made

not by models whose Madison Avenue pitches are as transparent as day but, instead, by real folks, with real accents and ordinary looks, who repeat the message over and over and over again, to the point that suspicions about the integrity of the product and its ability to perform as promised are replaced by a desire to buy. Buy. *Buy!*

When you think about it, this is where the "info" part of the word "infomercial" comes into play. The infomercial creators recognize that one of the most powerful ways to convince people to try their product or service is to provide them with what appear to be hard facts supporting the value proposition. In fact, the infomercials often make a subtle shift from advertising to quasi-journalism that reports on the product being offered, as opposed to providing a series of promotional scripts and jingles. This approach—best known as "educating the consumer"—keeps defense mechanisms in check and increases the likelihood of a sale.

Welcome to Wonderland

So look what we have learned: Yes, infomercials are cheesy and violate many of the "sophisticated" marketing rules such as "No one is going to sit through a sixty-minute commercial." And yet they work. Like a bulldog, they remain relentlessly focused on making a sale.

So we are faced with a paradox of marketing: Most everything the textbooks teach is the inverse of what actually works in the marketplace. Remember "Nothing happens until someone sells something"? Infomercial makers understand the importance of this. The infomercial is a hard-core, well-thought-out, carefully orchestrated sales job. Yes, they are tacky. But what do you want—to win awards, or to win business?

If that question offends your sense of ethics, or aesthetics, or morality, then maybe you shouldn't be in business. Because no matter what you are trying to market, the end result has to be the consummation of a sale. Everything else is just schmoozing and talking and singing and dancing and laughing and joking and wasting time, with no return on investment.

The infomercial makers were among the first to recognize the power of truly original thinking . . . of breaking the rules . . . of using imagination.

They didn't accept that commercials had to be thirty or sixty seconds long, that spokespeople had to be celebrities or model-pretty, or that you couldn't ask people to buy what you have to sell right then and there.

And they recognized that beating the competition's marketing for the sake of winning awards is a dumb waste of time. To these Extreme Marketers, the only goals are to get you to go to your wallet to get your credit card, make a phone call, and place an order. Every marketing campaign that forgets this primary focus *sucks*.

When infomercial pioneer Ron Popeil set out to sell his Veg-O-Matic food slicer and dicer, he didn't seek to create print ads more attractive than those of the makers of the kitchen tools he was competing with. Instead, he thought about human behavior and how he could leverage its dynamics to achieve his business goals. The classic kitchen item became a career high point for one of the most successful creators of infomercials, one who has been going strong for nearly a half century.

Popeil, like all good Extreme Marketers, is relentlessly creative. He didn't start by looking at what everyone else was doing—he forged his own path. You should, too.

Raising the bar

Everyone can be more creative. But it requires work.

First, you need to change your aim. Anyone can create a slightly better product, or a sort of interesting marketing campaign, but what fun is that? Steve Jobs had it right when he talked about his vision of Apple Computer: "We are going to change the world." If that's too poetic for you, adopt Bill Gates's way of thinking. His initial vision for Microsoft? "We are going to put a computer on every desk and in every home." If you aim high, you will be forced to think more creatively.

(It's interesting when you think about it. Gates and Tom Watson have a lot in common. Yes, of course, they built great technology-based companies, but their real genius may be as marketers. Watson focused on the importance of getting the sale. And Gates's major insight was in understanding the importance of a brand name. From the beginning, he set out to make Microsoft *the standard* when it came to software.)

Okay, you are not going to think like everyone else. You are going to set your sights high. Is there anything else you can do to increase the odds that what you come up with will be creative? Absolutely, and it takes us full circle: Challenge everything that has been accepted as a standard practice.

Every company has an established way of doing business. I am not talking about the human-resources manual that says you get three personal days annually, and four hours once a year to take your dog to the vet. I am talking about the company's standard operating systems and beliefs, and you should question each and every one of them. The vast majority of people accept these standard operating beliefs as the Holy Grail. People who succeed don't.

For example:

- Everyone knew that low-rated bonds were a terrible investment. Why do you think they called them "junk" bonds? But Michael Milken, a young man at the time, was the first person to challenge that successfully. He looked at the traditional default rate on junk bonds compared to corporate and treasury bonds and concluded that low-rated bonds were worth the risk. He transformed the way business was financed in the 1980s and into the 1990s.

* Everyone knew that you could not use the word "lemon" in a new-car ad. But the Doyle Dane Bernbach advertising agency did it anyway. It showed a picture of a brand-new VW Beetle with a huge, one-word headline: "Lemon." The juxtaposition got everyone to read the copy, which said that the car pictured had been rejected by VW's quality inspectors because of an internal cosmetic blemish that most people wouldn't have noticed. "If they take their inspections that seriously, maybe this is a pretty good car," people concluded. VW sales soared.

* Everyone knows that a key in retailing is cutting your costs to the bone. Yet one of our clients rewards store managers who have the *highest* electric bills. He wants his stores lit up twenty-four hours a day so that people can see what he sells. He considers it cheap advertising.

Real achievers question "the manual" and the accepted approaches, in order to divine better ways of accomplishing their goals and objectives.

If you start challenging the way things always have been done, you will take a position analogous to the financial world's concept of *zero-based budgeting*. That's where the budget for next year starts at $0 and each person has to justify requests for every single dollar, even if her program has been in place for decades.

In your case, rather than accepting the common wisdom, you will ask yourself repeatedly: *Is there a better way of doing what I have been told to do, or what others do by rote?*

Think of this approach as Serial Skepticism.

As you seek to improve your ranking on the Serial Skepticism scale, take the following steps:

- ► When you are asked to engage in any task according to a prescribed method, ask yourself if there is a better way of performing the activity.

- ► When someone makes a purported statement of fact—"E-mail marketing would never work for us"—ask yourself if it is really fact or fantasy. If your knee-jerk response is to say "fact," demand (of yourself) that you find a way to support the "fact."

- ► If you are inclined to trust someone's information, intentions, or motives, question your reaction by asking if he will gain more by misleading you than by sharing his knowledge with you.

If you start with a blank piece of paper and question everything you have ever heard, you will be substantially ahead of the competition.

4. Make a spectacle of yourself—or your company

Stop playing it safe with singles and doubles and start hitting home runs

PROBLEM

You aren't certain what tack your marketing should take in terms of humor/pathos/shock value/sex appeal/competitive attack.

SOLUTION

Always, always, always go to extremes to get people to fall in love with your product/service.

BENEFIT

Memorable marketing that drives sales.

RULE

Remember the original *Star Trek*? The creators got it right. You want "to boldly go where no man [or woman] has gone before." Otherwise, what fun is it going to work?

Think of it this way: You can play it safe and shoot for modest gains. The "slow and steady wins the race" crowd will tell you that if you can pump up sales by 10 percent a year, your company will double in size in slightly more than seven years.

That certainly is one road to take, but it's not the one I'd choose. I'd identify an opportunity and go after it with all guns blazing. That's because the *slow but steady* cliché often places you in an armchair, passively watching the winners race by.

Lou Gerstner understood this when he joined IBM in 1993. The outside consensus was that he had signed on to preside over its continued dissolution into a confederation of autonomous business units. This strategy was well under way when he arrived.

Instead, Gerstner decided to assume the daunting challenge of turning around the beleaguered IBM, which was suffering from decades of complacency, arrogance, and a lack of leadership that had produced a bloated bureaucracy unable to do the key things that grow successful companies: identify opportunities, develop appropriate product/service offerings, and effectively market and sell the right products/ services at the right price. Instead, the once-vaunted industry leader and innovator had become a big blue elephant, addicted to producing inconsequential two-hundred-page internal reports on just about everything that had nothing to do with selling technology.

So when Gerstner came along as the CEO, the inner circle he inherited suggested strongly that he develop a new and improved IBM mission statement. Given that the company had in fact lost its way and was groping for direction, that seemed to be a (slow but steady) sound idea.

It wasn't, and Gerstner knew it. He understood, given IBM's culture, that if he created a new mission statement, people inside the firm would spend the next two years debating it. So he rejected the suggestion out of hand.

Instead of doing the safe thing, the approach you might have expected, Gerstner did what was appropriate, which in this case was a bold move. He found a void in the technology market, and he filled it by marshaling IBM's consulting capabilities into a tightly knit, highly incentivized organization, which then went after the thousands of high-margin information-technology consulting contracts that were waiting to be plucked from corporate America.

In Gerstner's version of Extreme Marketing, he threw out all the standard IBM garbage—everything backed up in writing, artful internal PowerPoint presentations, and, above all, achieving consensus with your peers inside the company—and replaced it with a sales-focused culture that found a lucrative niche and cultivated it with great drive and skill.

Gerstner knew that he couldn't declare that "from this day forward there will be a new IBM." He had to show everyone—internally and externally—what would change. And he did that by getting rid of people who were inwardly focused—employees who spent all their time trying to figure out how they could satisfy their bosses—and replaced them with people who would be paid for satisfying the customer.

From day one, he focused on filling a void, a vacuum in the marketplace. And IBM's marketing—most notably its advertising—moved from "play it safe" technobabble to an edgy approach that put corporate America's confusion about technology, and its place inside companies, right into the crosshairs and proclaimed, "We have the answers."

Let me exaggerate to make a point. It's interesting, but everyone in business (well, virtually everyone) seems to run in the same direction, saying the same things, to the same prospective customers in the same banal/superficial/noncompelling way. Lazy Marketing! Lazy Marketing! This traditional approach is something that you need to battle at every turn.

Case in point: When the premier accounting and consulting firm Pershing Yoakley & Associates asked me to assess its marketing tools and initiatives, I summarized my findings to the executive team in two words: "It sucks."

The primary problem was that the company's marketing had not kept up with the company itself. While Pershing Yoakley had been founded twenty years before as the typical CPA firm serving a wide variety of clients, over time it had migrated from accounting to consulting, and had developed a particular expertise in working with health-care firms. In fact, by the time management called me, some 80 percent of the company's revenues and earnings were coming from the health-care industry, something you would never know from its marketing, which continued to portray Pershing Yoakley as a traditional accounting firm. There was no way to tell from the company's website, brochure, and other marketing material that it was one of the premier health-care-industry consulting firms in the nation.

As we have talked about before, it is vitally important that your marketing stress the one thing your company does better than anything else.

Working with Pershing Yoakley's management, we were able to summarize the firm's competitive advantage in a single sentence: "We provide an integrated suite of strategic and financial solutions for the health-care industry."

Just how important this was came to light a couple of months later. A Pershing Yoakley partner went to call on a very busy CEO prospect. After keeping him waiting for more than thirty minutes, the CEO brusquely said, "You have five minutes to tell me why my firm should hire you."

"I don't need five minutes," the partner said. "Just thirty seconds." And he proceeded to explain that Pershing Yoakley "provides an integrated suite of strategic and financial solutions for health-care companies just like yours." That got the CEO's full attention. Instead of five minutes, they had a two-hour meeting.

All of your marketing must be created so that it can be reduced to a single sentence. If it can't be, your message will be lost in the shuffle. Very few companies are this focused on their marketing. More the reason *you* should be.

If everyone is zigging, there's a huge opportunity if you zag

I learned about the importance of going a different way growing up in Queens, New York. I loved basketball, and every day after school my friends and I would gather on the blacktop behind the junior high and play until the janitor locked the gates at 6 P.M. The problem was that even though we had played for hours, we didn't want to quit at six.

One day as the janitor came out at 5:55 to begin shooing us away, I went up to him and said, "Look, lock us in. Don't worry. We'll get out when we're done."

He looked skeptical but agreed and put the padlock on the outside of the fence, locking us in on the playground.

We thought this was the greatest thing ever and played until dusk.

When we finally couldn't see anymore, it was time to go home, and my first thought was that maybe telling the janitor to lock us in wasn't the best idea. The fences surrounding the court were twenty feet high. (I guess they were afraid someone was going to come in the middle of the night and steal the backboards.) The only way out was to climb the fence.

My friends and I learned an important lesson that night. Climbing up twenty feet is easy; it is getting down in the near dark that's hard. Everyone ended up with ripped pants and bruised ribs, and there were a couple of sprained ankles.

I went home and realized we needed to do something differently. We could either leave by six, as everyone else did, or find a better alternative to risking our necks getting out of the place every night.

The next day, I came to school with wire cutters and a small can of green paint. With my friends shielding me from view, I cut a large-enough section out of the fence to make it easy for us to get out, and then we put it back in place and painted it over, so no one could tell what I had done.

From then on, we could come and go as we pleased. Safely. Much later, I realized that the way we went about ensuring more playing time could serve as a model for business success:

- ► Be imaginative
- ► Accept risk
- ► Assume challenges
- ► Find a new way to win

How others do it

We've talked about how a big company—IBM—took a bold step by ignoring the crowd, and how my friends and I did it when we were younger. Now let's look at how two mid-size companies, in different industries, handled it.

During the last thirty years, tens of thousands of co-ops and condominium properties have been built and/or converted across the nation.

The residence owners establish a board to manage the property and to look after their interests in a collective fashion. The board, in turn, hires a firm to manage the condominium/co-op property.

The management firm is charged with the responsibility of making certain that the common areas are well kept, that the heating and air-conditioning systems function properly, and that the building(s) is safe and secure.

In order to win new business, management firms must compete against each other to convince new and existing boards that they are superior to the competition. But just like advertising cars (pictures of long, winding roads) and retirement planning (couples walking into the sunset), here, too, the messages are all virtually the same:

We are a wonderful firm composed of wonderful people who care about your wonderful properties, and if you hire us you'll feel wonderful and life will be wonderful ever after.

Even though that is the tack that nearly every firm in the business has blindly and predictively pursued, it is not really a way to market to the condo/co-op boards. In fact, it is yet another example of marketing that sucks.

Condo/co-op boards, and the residents/owners they represent, have goals they want to achieve. Goals that are critically important to them. Goals that they measure management firms against. The management firm that speaks to these goals gains a huge competitive advantage.

Take the case of Yonkers, New York–based Prime Locations, Inc. Once the firm decided that it would go on an all-out mission to increase the number of co-op/condo properties it represented from forty-eight to a hundred, it utilized Extreme Marketing to accomplish this objective. And as management did, it figured out the sweet spot in the market that could command the attention of the boards. That is reflected in the company's simple but compelling message: "PLI Increases Property Values."

Think of the wisdom of this. Board members are property owners themselves and are voted into office by their fellow owners. At the end of the day, everyone's primary concern regarding the real estate they own is that it increase in value over time. Should they want to trade up, trade down, relocate, or simply cash in, the higher the value of the property, the greater their personal wealth.

A management firm that can do more than keep things tidy, secure, and well-functioning, one that can actually increase the value of the property, is a slam-dunk choice for the board. Positioning PLI as the firm that *increases property values* says what no one else is saying, and it says something that has enormous meaning and value to decision makers empowered to hire management firms.

Proving it

Extreme Marketers know enough not to simply make idle statements. They recognize the importance of backing up their claims with a strong value proposition that gives credence and force to their competitive advantage.

That is precisely what Prime Locations did. Utilizing Extreme Marketing, the company explained how it was able to increase property values. Specifically, it repeatedly hammered home three key points:

1. PLI understands real-estate finance and can play a significant role in restructuring a condo's/co-op's capital

structure. This can have a major impact on cash flow, operating expenses, and ultimately equity values. PLI's strength in financial know-how emanates from its ownership as well as management of real estate.

2. The company takes pride in its ability not only to maintain but to improve common areas through its innovative use of both landscaping and lighting. Properties that are not only safe but attractive fetch a higher resale value.

3. Equally important, the company points to its years of experience that help it to spot small problems—say, a leaky boiler—before they become big ones.

PLI's approach is a perfect example of Extreme Marketing at work: While virtually every other management firm is running toward the doorway that bears some boring message about "wonderful people taking care of wonderful people," PLI fills the void by communicating and delivering a vastly superior service measured in terms of dollars and cents. No wonder the number of buildings under its management is constantly climbing.

Bold means bold

As we have seen throughout, Extreme Marketing takes an entrepreneurial perspective that demands a measurable return on the investment dollars allocated to the marketing process. Extreme Marketers are both strategic and tactical. They identify opportunities—often considered inappropriate or impossible to cultivate by others—and pursue them vigorously. In fact, they never accept the notion that something cannot be done because it has not been done in the past.

Perhaps the best example of this is Herb Darwin Vest. A small-town Texas CPA, Vest served with the U.S. Army in Vietnam, volunteering over and over again for the most dangerous assignments—which earned him the Silver Star. He was wounded in the process and was awarded the Purple Heart.

When Vest returned from the war and resumed his accounting practice, it struck him that his clients paid much larger fees to the people to whom he referred them to help them manage their personal finances than they paid to Vest, their CPA, to prepare their tax returns. For example, when a client needed an investment professional to manage his money, Vest would introduce him to a Merrill Lynch broker in town who would stand to make commissions of tens of thousands of dollars or more, while Vest had to settle for professional fees.

Determined to put an end to this inequity, Vest decided to create a new company, H. D. Vest Financial Services, that would license CPAs, such as himself, to sell investment products to their clients. With this single stroke, CPAs who could actually sell, or who could find financial-services salespeople to partner with, would be freed from the yoke of hourly billing and would be able to benefit from the much greater potential of commission-based compensation.

But one major obstacle stood between Vest and the emergence of his business. At the time, CPAs were forbidden from accepting commissions, both on the national level by the American Institute of Certified Public Accountants (AICPA) and by state CPA societies as well. So although the idea seemed to be a stroke of genius—it was intuitively obvious that people would entrust their personal financial affairs to their most respected advisors—the rules in place would not allow those advisors to earn the commissions that were at the core of the Vest concept.

Undaunted, Herb Vest, the Extreme Marketer, promptly joined forces with the Federal Trade Commission, suing the AICPA for restraint of trade. Vest won his case, and the AICPA was forced to drop its ban on CPAs accepting commissions.

Vest then had to take on the state accounting societies, which for the most part remained adamant on the commission issue. The accounting societies believed that taking commissions would jeopardize a CPA's traditional role as an independent and objective advisor. But once again Vest was resolute. He began to sue in state courts, knocking down the laws one by one in domino fashion, as the state courts ruled in his favor.

While his fellow CPAs were engaged in Lazy Marketing 101—trying to outdo each other in promising clients that they were brilliant and dedicated professionals, but professionals who concentrated only on taxes and accounting—Vest decided to take a dramatically different tack, marketing his firm and the practices of the CPAs who got licensed with H. D. Vest Financial Services as unique entities that would serve clients' needs in a novel fashion.

Instead of turning to product-pushing stockbrokers and insurance agents, clients could now turn to their CPAs (whom they knew best and trusted most) to give them not only advice and guidance but the products they needed to achieve their financial goals.

Vest filled one of the countless market voids waiting for someone with entrepreneurial drive and Extreme Marketing.

By addressing legal issues and challenging them one by one, Vest began a new industry and built a highly successful company that licensed nine thousand CPAs to conduct sales and accept commissions. The payoff for his extreme vision and marketing skills? A $127 million jackpot, the amount of money that Wells Fargo paid in 2001 to buy out H. D. Vest Financial Services.

The point here is simple and has two parts:

1. If you are going to be bold, there should be no self-imposed limits.
2. Extreme Marketing—anything that helps grow revenues, profits, and equity value—pays extreme dividends.

5. There are no one-trick ponies

Who says synergy never works? The practical benefits of integrated marketing

PROBLEM

You have started spending dollars, perhaps lots of them, on a specific form of marketing: advertising, direct mail, public relations, whatever. But the needle has barely budged when it comes to increasing your sales or earnings.

SOLUTION

Rethink the linear, one-off approach you are taking. One marketing tactic rarely works by itself on a stand-alone basis. (You probably *don't* have to spend more money. But you probably do have to spend the money differently, using an integrated set of marketing tools and initiatives.

BENEFIT

One marketing tactic will reinforce the other, making the campaign greater than the sum of its parts; you will have released the power of synergy.

RULE

As countless studies have shown, corporate mergers designed to achieve operating "synergy" usually fail. However, attempts at capturing the power of marketing synergies within a business often succeed.

Congratulations! After years of research, your company has finally developed On-Off, the first software tracking program that lets you tell at a glance what computer programs everyone in a company is using and how often they are using them.

This is a major breakthrough. Organizations pay substantial licensing fees to software companies so that their employees can benefit from such products as Lotus Notes. But what if a significant portion of those "licensed" employees never use the product? If management was aware of this—and this was an extremely big "if" until On-Off came along—it could reduce the number of licensees it pays for. On-Off was therefore filling a huge void and was destined to become a hot product.

Convinced it is about to take the world by storm, On-Off's management develops an advertising campaign, meant to run in software and information-technology journals, designed to tell the world about what the company has created. There are cool pictures of the On-Off box (the software itself looks like yet another CD), customer testimonials, product guarantees, and suggestions that IT department managers buy *the next big thing* at "once-in-a-lifetime prices." They put the product on the shelves and cross their fingers that the investment they have made in the On-Off ad campaign will generate a windfall in revenues, profits, and ultimately corporate valuation.

They can't be certain of the results, of course, but one thing On-Off's senior executives do know for sure: *They are engaged in the process of marketing.*

Well, not so fast.

All they are really doing is advertising. Spending money. Creating ads. Buying media. Almost every costly failure in the business world has done that (squared).

Think back to Super Bowl XXXIV in 2000 and the blizzard of dot-com commercials that were ooooh sooooo clever and creative and cool and . . . didn't do a damn thing to grow a business. Most of the companies behind those ads (and the marketing "geniuses" who authorized them) are now permanent members of the Business Hall of Shame.

There was a total of thirty-six advertisers for the Super Bowl between the St. Louis Rams and the Tennessee Titans, a game that was literally not decided until the last play. The Rams won 23–16.

But while the game was memorable, the ads were not. Of those thirty-six advertisers, seventeen—that's 47 percent—were dot-com companies. Those fledgling companies, most losing money, spent on average $2.2 million to buy thirty seconds of airtime during the game, and hundreds of thousands of dollars more to produce the ads.

What did they get for that money? Apparently, not much. Do you remember ads from Agillion.com (personalized Web pages), Kforce.com (a job site), or OurBeginning.com (online stationery)?

These were very, very expensive wastes of money. For example, Computer.com (it provided online advice and technical support for computer users) spent a total of $2.7 million for two ads during the pre-game plus one in the fourth quarter. And that does not include the production costs. Those numbers come courtesy of TheStreet.com, which pointed out that the ads consumed just about half of Computer.com's start-up capital.

Most of the dot-coms that advertised during Super Bowl XXXIV are now out of business, have merged into another entity, or now have a different business focus.

Okay, so they swung and missed. But I hear you ask: Isn't my suggestion of putting them in the Hall of Shame going a bit too far? Weren't they just businesspeople who suffered from the very human tendency to be overly exuberant about a new concept and embrace it as if it were the Holy Grail?

Perhaps—but that's not what they (or you) are paid to do.

Running a company isn't the same as taking an M.B.A. course, in which the worst thing that happens is you get an

F on your term paper. This is BUSINESS! Careers, dollars, dividends, and reputations are on the line. Here, the law of the jungle is devastatingly simple: Engage in marketing that sucks, and dollars get vacuumed into a black hole. And worse than that (yes, it can get much worse), companies fail. Jobs are lost. Shareholders sue. The media finds a scapegoat and ravages the son of a bitch (who finds it hard to find another job), and then the process starts all over again. Next company. Next victim.

But it doesn't have to be that way. Although the perception of marketing being a spend-and-run tactic is common throughout the business community—from the Fortune 500 to start-ups like On-Off—that view is based on a faulty premise. Specifically:

It is ludicrous to believe that engaging in any single component of marketing—be it advertising, public relations, sales promotion, or direct mail—amounts to a marketing program.

Instead, it is a single-action crapshoot that is likely to fail precisely because it is not supported by a full complement of marketing initiatives that must reinforce one another, producing a powerful synergy that makes $2 + 2 = 5$.

At this point, you may ask, "Isn't advertising On-Off better than doing nothing at all?" That's not the issue. A wiser approach is to ask what can be done to support the investment in advertising so that On-Off can achieve its financial objectives. This requires an integrated set of marketing tools and initiatives carefully constructed within the framework of a multifaceted marketing campaign.

To do that, you must create a blueprint designed to make sure that all of your marketing tactics work together.

Before discussing what you should do, let's make sure you know what to avoid so that you don't waste either time or money. Marketing that sucks—that is, marketing that fails to produce a significant return on the marketing dollars spent—can be traced to a series of factors that tend to be repeated ad infinitum. Consider the following four factors to be:

A checklist of common Lazy Marketing mistakes

Mistake #1: Create a budget first, goals second. (If at all.)

Consider this all-too-common scenario: Titan Technologies has decided that it will address a sluggish sales environment by increasing its marketing. Even though the economy is barely moving, the company isn't going to pull back.

This, often, *is* a good idea. Even if sales are slow during an economic downturn, they never stop altogether. And if everyone else is cutting back on spending during a recession, as is frequently the case, it can be an opportunity for you to gain market share by being aggressive. So the decision to increase spending may be a good one. But this is what a fly on the wall would have heard at the company's kickoff meeting.

Titan's president, Kathy Sound: We all know sales are down. And we all know that we cannot accept that. Orders are declining. Inventories are mounting. Morale is suffering. Titan is a can-do company, and in that spirit, we are going to act. So I am here today to announce that we will spend one million dollars on marketing this year—far more than we have ever spent before. (CHEERS AND APPLAUSE FROM THE TITAN MANAGEMENT AND EMPLOYEES.)

Titan's marketing VP, Rich Holland: Great news, Kathy. I knew you would come up with the masterstroke.

CFO Donna Hunt: And at a budget figure we can live with. Bravo!

Bravo, nonsense. Think about it. Titan has decided how much money it will spend—and the management team falls quickly in line behind the figure—before anyone in the company has bothered to figure out

a. How Titan will use marketing to grow out of its sales slump
b. Who the target of its marketing campaign will be

c. The messages it will use to position Titan as *the* customer solution

d. What the marketing blueprint will look like

e. What goals it will seek to achieve

f. How the campaign will be measured

g. How leads will be captured

h. How Titan is going to test, execute, and monitor the results (we will talk more about this in Chapter 7).

When the applause stops, and reality sets in, Titan will realize that it has deepened its financial woes by committing to a $1 million marketing budget in the blind. Management will spend big money without any clear plan for how it will generate additional revenues for the business.

This "putting the budget before the goals" is a near-sure way to create a money-wasting marketing plan that sucks.

Mistake #2: Be a one-day wonder.

If Kathy Sound is like many of her peers in the management ranks, she will prove to be a one-day wonder. Once she makes the "brave new world" announcement that her company is turning up the heat on its marketing efforts, she will retreat from the front, leaving her troops to hire the agency, spend the dollars, make the blunders, chase their tails—and all too often, make her company $1 million poorer with nothing much to show for it.

The fact is, as we will explore in detail later in this chapter, that great marketing takes great leadership and execution. Specifically, the leader must

- ► Create the vision ("We need a marketing plan to do X")
- ► See that the plan is executed well
- ► Make sure the marketing is working

Whether the company is a start-up or an industrial giant, senior management's involvement/support/commitment is essential.

Think of how Dave Thomas immersed himself in Wendy's advertising, to the point that his "everyman" personality became a metaphor for the company's "good food at fair prices" value proposition. You never could picture him in the mansion he must have lived in. All you remember is a dorky-looking guy in a short-sleeved shirt and tie, seated like any other customer in a Wendy's (a restaurant you somehow knew he named after his daughter). And once the commercial was over, you were left with the distinct impression that Dave—in a million years, you would never think of calling him Mr. Thomas—wouldn't allow you to be served a bad hamburger or have a bad experience in his restaurant.

This fusion of leader + marketing + company helped to turn Wendy's from a money-hemorrhaging McDonald's wanna-be to a fast-food leader.

Now, think of how you see most CEOs in ads: Bill Ford

in the Ford spots; Auggie Busch IV for Budweiser. Their hair is perfect. They are wearing makeup, and they appear in a sterile environment. Do those spots move product? Do you truly believe that these executives are intimately involved in their company's marketing campaigns, or was it just something fun to do between board meetings?

Mistake #3: Delegate.

Equally bad is the chief executive who is completely hands-off. Take the president of an $8 million-a-year software company—with big plans for an IPO—who carried the flag for the company's clever and tightly integrated marketing program until the firm landed $20 million in venture capital.

Up until then, he set the direction of the marketing plan ("I want us to be positioned as *the* company whose software makes managers smarter"), made sure the message was communicated effectively (by signing off on all ads), and held the marketing department responsible for the success of their campaigns ("If we don't generate revenues that are at least two times what this new marketing program costs, I want it killed. Immediately").

The campaign was a huge success, powering sales and raising the company's profile to the point where it could attract significant venture-capital funding.

At that point, the chief executive made the decision that he would change from being an entrepreneur to becoming the builder of a budding bureaucracy. He began focusing exclusively on the dynamics of reporting systems and internal controls. Although he was a sales-and-marketing whiz who had built the company from the ground up in less than three years, he suddenly decided that *all* his time should be spent building an internal organization.

Wham. He delegated marketing to functionaries who could go through the motions of creating brochures, websites, and the like, but who were clueless about the alchemy it takes to turn these elements into a powerful sales-building tour de force. No wonder revenues and earning increases slowed to a crawl in the aftermath of the transition.

Mistake #4: The gullibility factor.

Marketing agencies that aren't worth their salt (in other words, those that can't turn advertising, public relations, direct mail, and other initiatives into sales) know how bad they are. But they don't admit it—hey, they're marketers.

Instead, they dish out shovelfuls of nonsense that marketing is all about image making. They will insist that although you can't measure the performance of what they do, you should rest assured that your company's image is improving, thanks to hiring them, and somehow, someday—in some invisible, intangible, and unintelligible fashion—it will pay dividends.

Garbage! If you hear such doubletalk from an agency pitching for your business, demand that they leave. Immediately. Not only is it possible to design marketing so that the initiatives and tools you create can generate customer relationships (and ultimately sales), it is near criminal to accept anything less.

What you are looking for in an agency—or in a candidate to run your marketing department—is that they understand the importance of integrating all of your marketing tactics.

In the next chapter, we will go through a case study of how that should work in practice.

Leadership: painting pictures that motivate teams

Marketing leadership requires these traits:

The ability to paint a picture of what the marketing will accomplish.

Actually, this is the inverse of Kathy Sound's (all-too-common) approach. Instead of claiming the bragging rights to a big budget ("We will spend X million dollars on marketing"), this leadership approach starts by talking about what the marketing must deliver. "We will gain another twelve percent of the hiking-boot market, taking the top spot among the eighteen- to-thirty-five-year-old segment"; or "Our website will be the first place people turn to when they are thinking about retirement planning."

To make sure the goals are achieved, it is always a good idea to make sure that the people doing your marketing have "skin in the game." When he was turning around IBM, Lou Gerstner made sure that every senior manager's salary was tied directly to sales and earnings.

The determination to monitor the logistics and measure the results.

Golf pros will tell you that one "drives for show and putts for dough." In marketing, this translates into the need to combine the aesthetic and the strategic.

Making powerful advertisements—and extremely creative collateral material like brochures and websites—is important because strong visuals and compelling text can move people to switch brands/try a new product/purchase more goods and services. But all is lost if the logistics are given short shrift.

For example, you have to monitor

- ► Where the ads are placed
- ► How often are they placed
- ► How long they run on radio and TV
- ► How well they work with your public relations and other tactical steps (remember, you want each aspect of a campaign to reinforce the other)

You then need to put in place metrics that can track how well you are succeeding toward your goal of increasing market share or achieving your unique position in the local, national, or global marketplace. Fall asleep at the wheel here, and your marketing—no matter how good the creative may be—will fail.

Case in point: When an upscale community of second homes located in a second-tier Florida city sought to attract buyers, the company placed advertisements in newspapers and radio stations that had upscale demographics in the Northeast. Given that communities like Greenwich, Connecticut, Westchester County, New York, and Bergen County, New Jersey, have a burgeoning number of aging baby boomers with money, the strategy seemed on target. In turn, the company spent hundreds of thousands of dollars on this "sure thing."

When the returns (measured in leads) turned out be consistently disappointing, management took the knee-jerk reaction of simply upping the budget.

Again.

And again.

Only after the well ran dry, and the CFO demanded answers, did the "marketing team" discover that targeting rich baby boomers in the Northeast was a costly dead end.

Why? No one bothered to ask the kindergarten question: *Will rich people who live in one place buy a second home in another that is located in a community perceived to be less desirable than where they are living now?*

What if—I mean WHAT THE HELL IF—the answer is no? Then the entire strategy and tactics and the dollars to support it would come to naught.

And the answer proved to be no! People wouldn't buy second homes in a place that was seen as less upscale than their primary residence. Buying within the second-tier city was seen not as a logical extension of their lifestyle but as an embarrassing *(Did we suddenly get poor? Is this the best we can do?)* step down in the social and economic hierarchy—a fact the "marketers" never bothered to discern.

The lessons here are as simple as they are obvious.

a. Blind marketing—marketing without context—is just stupid. It makes no sense to try to sell well-off people something that will make them feel less than well-off. (Would you try to sell diapers to a family without kids?)

b. What follows from that is you want to ask people why they *didn't* buy from you. A few phone calls to Greenwich, Connecticut, or Scarsdale, New York, would have revealed that the marketing campaign was fatally flawed. Residents of these upscale communities would have made it clear that they wouldn't buy a second home in any place that wasn't equally upscale as their legal residence. Overlooking why you didn't get the business is a common—and critical—mistake. Stand outside your store and look for people who leave empty-handed, or use technology tools such as cookies (which track visitors to your website) and then e-mail people who came to your website but left without buying, and ask them why they didn't make a purchase. You are trying to discover what you can do differently in the future in order to make them do business with you. Remember, focusing on your company's "closing rate" is often not as important as scrutinizing its "failure to close rate." No matter how many people are buying, when you see that people are leaving your store empty-handed (or visiting your website and not buying or meeting with your sales force without signing a purchase order), red lights should start flashing. Take the time to figure out what you need to improve.

c. If the leader doesn't get involved in the details, the company can end up losing a lot of money.

The staying power to remain committed throughout the course of the campaign.

All too often, marketing sucks because it doesn't have the time to work.

It takes *time* to make people dream, change their minds, think about issues, and explore new products. This doesn't happen when companies engage in blink-of-an-eye campaigns that must prove themselves with immediately measurable results or they will be replaced by another quick-fix scheme that won't do anything (except waste more dollars).

Virtually all of the world's great companies were slow-brewed. Their founders were part scientists and engineers and accountants and technologists, but they were also instinctive marketers. They created a brand and a method of marketing and stayed with it, allowing the message to resonate and their products to satisfy and word of mouth to kick in. Virtually every enduring company was built this way. We've already talked about how IBM's Tom Watson and Microsoft's Bill Gates were great marketers, but so, too, was James O. McKinsey, who had already had an established practice in budgeting and finance when he decided to test his new theory: that so-called management engineers could go beyond rescuing sick companies and could help healthy ones. So, in 1926, he formed a new firm—McKinsey & Co.—and sold his theory company by company and created a new industry, management consulting. And no one can doubt that discount-brokerage pioneer Charles Schwab is a great marketer. The list goes on and on.

Contrast this with the dot-coms that have vanished from the landscape like fireflies in winter. Yes, their business models sucked. Yes, they forgot that companies have to make money. And yes, these were central flaws in their architecture. But certainly one of their biggest flaws was their focus on big-budget, quick-hit marketing.

In the long run, the stay-the-course players (think Wal-

Mart) dominate by remaining focused on a message, such as Sam Walton's mantra, "We will have everyday low prices," and communicating that message relentlessly to customers. ("We are the low-price leader; we are the low-price leader.")

The willingness to create a tight alignment between the president's office and the marketing campaign.

Think of it this way: The CEO—of any company, be it a start-up or a Fortune 500 giant—is (or should be) the company's chief strategist. She develops and constantly tweaks/refines/adjusts plans to sell stuff, pirate customers from competitors, raise prices, increase profits, identify new kinds of prospects, and expand customer relationships. She knows the industry, the consumer, the competitors, and the economics of it all.

But in all too many cases, she either views marketing as ancillary to her job of running the company and so doesn't pay much attention to it, or—and this is frequently true—she doesn't know what it takes to construct a truly effective marketing campaign. In either case, she leaves the supervision of the company's marketing programs to someone else.

What a disconnect that is! It virtually assures that the company's marketing will be out of sync with the strategy—and that the marketing will suck.

No, the CEO does not have to be the chief marketing officer as well, but she definitely needs to be intimately involved in whatever is going on. If she isn't, serious problems—such as wasting the marketing budget—can easily follow.

What Phil and Rhonda did wrong

Consider the case of a small information-technology consulting firm owned and managed by Philip and Rhonda. They know servers. They know LANS. They know WANS. They eat technology for lunch. Breathe it. Dream about it.

No one can argue that it is a good thing for the leaders of a tech firm to be deeply immersed in technology. But there's deeply immersed and then there's *deeply immersed*—at the expense of everything else.

Even that wouldn't have been a problem until they decided to take what they knew best—technology—and apply it directly to their marketing program.

When it came time for them to launch a campaign to grow their company, they allocated $100,000—and basically threw it over the wall to "the marketers." Having authorized the expenditure, they went back to their techno-focus—an invitation to disaster.

Phil and Rhonda had developed a software program that turned high-powered workstations into something close to minicomputers.

The logical questions they needed to answer were:

- How do they want to position the company?
- What is their value proposition?
- What makes them a better choice than other tech consultants?
- What does their company stand for?

But Phil and Rhonda had no intention of spending time with the marketing "lightweights," the technologically challenged, in order to help figure out the positioning for the new product and how it should be advertised. And the so-called marketers never bothered to force Phil and Rhonda to answer the critical questions they needed to build an effective campaign. So they produced a website, a brochure, a PR campaign, and a direct-mail program that:

- **Had the wrong message.** They talked about the additional power that Phil and Rhonda's creation would give computers, instead of what users could do with the power.

- **Offered no strong reason to hire the firm.** Yes, they acknowledged that Phil and Rhonda had invented the product, but they downplayed the consultants' skill in being able to help every organization adapt their workstations in order to use it.

- **Were directed at non–decision makers.** The ads ran in "consumer" computer magazines, to underscore how cool the invention was, as opposed to magazines like *CIO* and *CIO Insight*, which target the people who have technology-budget authority: chief information officers.

- **FAILED TO PRODUCE A SINGLE CUSTOMER.**

In order for marketing to power a company's growth curve, for it to qualify as Extreme, it must originate from the leaders' strategy. Fortify it. Support it. Make it happen. Anything else is bound to suck.

6. Extreme Marketing in action

The last word on synergy and developing an integrated plan for making sure every marketing dollar you spend brings in more than $1 in return

PROBLEM

How do you transition from Lazy to Extreme Marketing?

SOLUTION

Integrate every part of your marketing. Create a plan that assures that every dollar you spend adds firepower to your marketing program, not just more zeros to the marketing budget.

BENEFIT

Each of your marketing components will reinforce the others.

RULE

7

Every marketing dollar you spend should not only generate more than $1 in return—it should help leverage all of your other marketing spending.

The purpose of this book is to get you and your company to move from traditional ("it sucks") marketing to Extreme Marketing.

Let's spend a few moments with a fictitious company that did just that.

After countless false starts that saw it waste more than $1 million on just about every marketing program you can think of, a Boston-based start-up finally got its act together. The company—we'll call it E-Closings—decided to create an integrated marketing program designed so that each component would reinforce the others. It proved to be the absolutely right way for the company to tell the world about its system, which allows you to conduct certain real-estate transactions online. Instead of being forced to drive to a bank or a lawyer's office, and sign endless legal documents, thanks to E-Closings you can handle the entire transaction electronically.

While the story has a happy ending, it took a long time to get there. Why? Because the founders had accepted all the conventional "wisdom" when it came to marketing— what supposedly worked and what didn't—and so it took a long time to change their minds. (The fact that they had lost $1 million trying to implement that conventional wisdom, and had found little but frustration as a result, made persuading them a bit easier.)

At the outset, the founding entrepreneurs—a twenty-nine-year-old techie with a computer-science degree from MIT and her partner, a numbers-crunching thirty-one-year-old Wharton M.B.A. with a near-religious faith in the power of financial projections—figured they would pursue what could be described as the Chinese-menu approach to marketing.

Because marketing for them was an afterthought at best, they figured they would lay out all their marketing choices as you find them listed on a Chinese menu—they placed some items, such as producing a brochure, in a column labeled "A" and other tactics, such as public relations, in a column labeled "B."

Then, seemingly at random, they would pick one approach from A, another couple from B, sprinkle in a dollop of networking in the real-estate industry, and presto! (from their naive perspective): An industry that adhered to a Dickensian methodology of having clients sign dozens of pieces of paper to complete a transaction would magically embrace the digital age.

Here we had the all-too-common case of smart people willing to press Delete on all their business knowledge and common sense when it came to marketing. Without knowing it, or giving it much thought, they were determined to squander more than $1 million in *marketing that sucks*. All they "knew" was that to be complete businesspeople they had to market their service, and they figured their approach was as good as any.

This led to an interesting and sometimes tense discussion when we were brought in and began to introduce the concept of Extreme Marketing.

Marketer: When you create software code, you
follow a certain carefully constructed logic, right?

MIT Techie: Of course. The process would break
down without that.

Marketer: Why is that the case?

Techie: Because all of the elements of a source code
are interrelated. If a single line of ten thousand
lines of code is out of whack, it is the equivalent of
the weakest link in a chain.

Marketer: It may come as a surprise to you, but the
same is true in marketing. You can acquire a series
of tools and put in place an array of initiatives, but
unless they are integrated, they do not produce
the kind of synergies that generate a high return
on investment.

Techie: Now it's my turn to ask you a question: Why
do you say that?

Marketer: Because marketing has logic and a pattern, too. And unless the components are made to fit together properly, you have that same weak-link effect as in source code. For example: If you advertise in *Real Estate News*, combined with a public-relations placement in that publication, the messages reinforce each other. To that, you can add a drive-to-Web offer in the ad—where you say, "Visit our website to learn more, and receive a discount"—and then offer both the discount and something else, like a booklet called *Ten Things to Make Your Real-Estate Transaction Go Smoothly*. Once they are at your website, you can entice them to give you all their contact information in order to receive the booklet. That way you can build a prospect/customer database.

As we noted, if you do all that, you are on your way to creating a powerful force that identifies, tracks, and sells prospects, and gives you the ability to cross-sell them over and over again. If your company takes this approach, then spending money on marketing makes sense. You are not doing things at random. Everything you do reinforces everything else.

If you allow us to be candid, what you are likely doing now—a little of this, a little of that—

doesn't make sense. Your à la carte approach is a way of spending money with little likelihood that you will ever recoup your investment, let alone triple or quadruple it.

Think of it this way: In marketing, we use the term *drip campaign.* This refers to a positive kind of water torture. It means that you keep getting your message out to the prospect/customer over and over again—in different formats and media— so that the message cuts through the clutter of competing messages and the reason to buy becomes clearer and stronger with each iteration.

When it comes to E-Closings, we want prospects to read an ad, receive an e-mail, notice a news story, peruse a sale promotion letter, visit the website, hear a testimonial . . .

This is how you convince people to change their habits and loyalties and buy your product or service, and how you get them to make follow-up purchases of upgrades and ancillary products.

Changing their ways

The case that the Extreme Marketers presented convinced the founding entrepreneurs to allocate their marketing budget to an integrated campaign that would:

1. Create a powerful message: "Finally, a twenty-first-century way to handle your real-estate transactions quickly, efficiently, and inexpensively"
2. Reinforce the message with repeated impressions in a variety of media
3. Link the message to special offers: "Receive a free booklet, plus 20 percent off if you act now"
4. Build credentials for the company and its service by establishing it as the leader in this new field
5. Attract and cross-sell customers

In the end, the new company adopted a comprehensive Extreme Marketing plan to accomplish those five objectives.

The first step was to establish an executive summary reflecting the company's core strategy. Here, too, the entrepreneurs objected, complaining that this was unnecessary because they could picture in their heads exactly what they were doing and where they were headed.

Precisely the point, we told them. Ask a businesswoman to present how her company distinguishes itself in the marketplace, and you will often find that the picture in her mind is much fuzzier, and less effective, than she thinks it is once she actually presents it.

Creating an executive summary forces the management team to crystallize its thinking and puts it to the acid test of subjecting it to the opinion of others—advisors, accountants, bankers, and venture capitalists. In many cases, this leads to a change in the company's approach, business model, or direction. As we have previously discussed, you want to crystallize your product offering so that people know exactly why they should do business with you.

By going through this exercise, you may discover that what you think you do for a living, and what your customers think you do, are two different things.

For example, we had a client that sold very-high-end pools—we're talking swimming pools that averaged $450,000 each. When asked to create an executive summary, the company wrote: "We create and install expensive pools."

Their customers, however, saw it differently: The pool was just part of the perfect home environment that the company helped to create.

As a result of that difference, the company started concentrating on the landscaping part of its business—something it just threw in to help show off its pools. Today, landscaping and lawn maintenance has become a significant part of the business.

The new positioning for the company is focused on the outdoor lifestyle. Its ads now use concepts such as "Escape!" and underscore how the company creates a seamless environment for the good life.

For E-Closings, the following positioning was created.

Executive Summary

E-Closings embodies a compelling business concept with the power to dramatically change the dynamics of an outdated and inefficient process that is critical to the real-estate industry. By helping to transition certain transactions from a manual, brick-and-mortar methodology to an e-commerce functionality, E-Closings can bring new efficiencies and generate a high return measured in

- *Accelerated turnaround time*
- *Increased productivity*
- *Less paperwork*

These benefits create an exceptional value proposition for key parties to the transactions, who will stand to benefit by purchasing access to E-Closings, using the company's service as a facilitator of the closing process and/or as a tool for improving the management and productivity of their businesses.

Clearly, a few paragraphs summarized not only the company's defining concept but also the value proposition it would bring to the marketplace.

This was not a static statement—it was a strategic mirror against which the company would hold all new ideas, plans, and proposed courses of action.

If a new suggestion failed to be in sync with the summary, the company would either (a) reject the new idea, plan, or proposed course of action, because it was outside the business model, or (b) revise the summary (assuming, of course, there was a compelling reason to do so).

Once the Executive Summary was complete, the marketers proceeded to help E-Closings achieve its full potential by launching the following plan of attack—one that can be adapted for virtually every kind of business.

STEP 1: BRANDING

Essential to E-Closings' success as a business is the company's ability to establish itself as a highly effective alternative to the current closing process and, related to this, as a widely recognized destination by key parties in the real-estate industry, including title companies, lawyers, real-estate agents, mortgage bankers, buyers, sellers, and home inspectors.

In short, what E-Closings is offering is unique, and for this reason the company, perhaps more than most, requires a distinct branding that is memorable and that resonates with these constituents/customers. The branding program includes the following three key elements:

► A logo, which provides a graphic depiction of the company's ability to facilitate closings online. The idea? You can tell at a glance what E-Closings does.

► A tag line, which conveys in a concise and creative

manner what the company does and how it delivers value to its customers. This is an opportunity that too many companies overlook. If you end every communication with "Fit Life Beef: The only beef that guarantees you will lose ten pounds a day," it will help reinforce what you stand for in the marketplace. The converse may be even more important. Every time you move away from your strongest asset, you are camouflaging what you have to sell.

► A design standard, including selected colors and type fonts that will govern the company's communications and provide a professional and memorable impression with every communication that the company does.

STEP 2: PUBLIC RELATIONS

E-Closings needed to become well recognized as an economically superior alternative to the traditional process of consummating certain real-estate transactions, and as a well-known real-estate industry destination on the Internet. This profile building had to be accomplished through a comprehensive and proactive media/public-relations campaign targeted to the key participants in the closing process, including

► Home buyers
► Home sellers
► Real-estate agents

- Owners and managers of real-estate agencies
- Title companies
- Home-inspection companies
- Mortgage bankers/real-estate lenders

Why was P.R. necessary? The advantage of public relations is that you are always leveraging the implicit endorsement of the media doing the story.

Consumers know that anyone can buy an ad. But to get a story done on a company, it must have been vetted, to some degree, by the reporter doing the piece. It appears—even when this is not the case—that the *New York Times*, CNN, or your local newspaper is heralding your business when it does a story about you or your company.

E-Closings is a new idea. All new ideas need endorsements by influential, disinterested third parties whose opinions will resonate with the prospective customers your company has targeted.

To reach this targeted group of the press (and the reporters and editors who work for them), the E-Closings campaign was directed at the following major types of media outlets:

- Real-estate magazines, newsletters, and newspapers
- Mortgage-banking magazines, newsletters, and newspapers

- Personal-finance publications and broadcast media
- Online publications focused on all of the above constituencies

The media/public-relations methodology for E-Closings adhered to the following process:

1. Identify the appropriate media outlets.

2. Target the appropriate contact names at those outlets.

3. Develop an immediate positioning strategy designed to serve as the focal point for news and feature-story ideas. The positioning must be for the reporters' benefit, not the client's. Reporters don't care about advancing your agenda. You need to convince them why what you have is a story. You need to explain why your product or service is innovative, contrarian, or a new concept.

   What might be examples of each? For one investment firm, we put a headline on a news release that read "Bulls, Bears, and Armadillos." Everyone knows that bull is the term for an optimist on Wall Street, and if you are negative you are a bear. But an armadillo? It was a term we coined for an investor who armed himself against a prickly stock market. That was intriguing to the media, and, as a result, the investment firm got substantial press coverage.

Contrarian is relatively simple. "Everybody thinks Z, but the answer is really A" is the way you pitch your story.

And E-Closings was certainly a new concept.

4. **Messaging.** E-Closings' key message—the ability to transition the real-estate industry from a brick-and-mortar system to a faster, more economically viable online process—was tweaked for each specific market segment, including property buyers, sellers, attorneys, title companies, real-estate agents, and mortgage bankers, depending on the publication targeted.

To make contact with the appropriate media representatives, and to develop favorable coverage, E-Closings used a media kit, including a series of press releases, a company backgrounder, case examples illustrating the ease of consummating transactions online, and material explaining the general economic benefit of transitioning to the virtual-closing-room concept.

Having little experience with public relations—in fact, confusing it with networking and other one-on-one activities—the entrepreneurs demanded that this initiative be eliminated from the Extreme Marketing plan. They objected to its cost—$100,000—which they believed could be put to better use in advertising, and because they didn't believe they could get their message out. They thought the media would have little interest in covering their fledgling company with the Ciscos and the Microsofts of the world competing for attention from the business press.

But the marketers recognized that the founders' view was myopic.

Here's how the exchange went.

Techie: Why do we want to commit a hundred thousand dollars to a program that may wind up with little or no media coverage, when we can put that money into the real-estate press, in the form of advertising, and know for sure that our message will be seen?

Marketer: First, advertising and public relations are not mutually exclusive. In fact, the best programs reinforce each other. There is a major advertising component to our plan, but before we get to that, keep this in mind: Precisely because it is viewed as *news* as opposed to *advertising*, the articles that we place through P.R. have much greater impact in the marketplace. P.R. provides a credibility factor that advertising—important as it will be to E-Closings—cannot provide.

If we engage in smart P.R.—well-designed and well-executed—we gain exponentially more coverage for the company than a hundred thousand dollars in advertising can buy. It is a card we must play.

In order to play it well, several key assets and initiatives needed to be incorporated into the media/public-relations program. For example, an advisory board of prominent real-estate individuals was recruited to endorse the E-Closings concept and to lend their credentials to the business. A series of pitch letters was created for media representatives, to be followed up by personalized telephone calls.

Eventually the founders relented. Given the press that E-Closings got, the P.R. campaign more than paid for itself.

Advertising

Although advertising is an essential component of an integrated marketing campaign, it is often the most costly element—a budget-buster unless it is carefully planned and placed within the framework of the overall strategic/marketing plan.

As is often the case with business executives who fail to grasp the totality of marketing, E-Closings' top managers wanted to allocate too much money to ad spending at the expense of the other elements—such as P.R. and direct mail—that would provide greater results for less dollars.

To rein them in, the Extreme Marketers established measurable goals for the ad campaign. Under this arrangement, ad spending could be approved only if it helped to accomplish four key objectives:

- Reinforce the message that E-Closings is a time-and cost-efficient alternative to the traditional method of consummating real-estate transactions. This message would be integral to the ad, or the ad wouldn't run.

- Build recognition for E-Closings and its value proposition among its prospective customers/users/referral sources. The marketers would measure that by checking on the name recognition for E-Closings before and after the ad ran. If name recognition didn't go up, the ad would be pulled.

- Establish www.e-closings.com as a significant destination for the real-estate community and for parties to real-estate transactions. Like the first point, this would be in the copy, or the ad wouldn't run.

- Generate sales leads. The marketers would do that by giving a specific phone number and URL for prospects to contact for more information. Ads in different publications had different phone numbers and URLs, so it would be easy to track exactly which ad generated which call or Web visit.

There are two points to underscore about this.

First, "creative types" within ad agencies won't like the restrictions put on the copy—that is, that it must continuously reinforce the core marketing message. That's too bad. As we have said throughout, your goal is to generate sales, not win advertising awards.

Second, don't make potential prospects do homework. A lot of times, an ad will say, "Be sure to mention Department B when you call." It is a way for the advertiser to track which ad triggered the call. It's far better to set up separate phone numbers that are associated with each media outlet where you advertise. That way, you are not requiring a prospect to do your work for you, and you get a more accurate response.

In the case of E-Closings' P.R. initiatives, the fact that the company was trying to reach distinct markets—real-estate attorneys, title companies, house inspectors, mortgage bankers, and real-estate agents—made it fairly easy to design a targeted advertising campaign. Ads ran in publications designed to reach each of those specific markets.

In each instance, the ads firmly established that E-Closings

- ► Was a revolutionary way to consummate real-estate transactions
- ► Used technology to save time and money
- ► Made all of the information about the transactions available on a 24/7 basis
- ► Saved everyone involved time and money

In addition to print advertising, the marketers convinced the company to place banner ads on key real-estate industry websites. Additionally, they prompted the company to test cable TV and radio advertising designed to serve as a lead generator for all segments of the E-Closings prospect universe, including property buyers and sellers, attorneys, title companies, real-estate agents, bankers, and inspectors.

This broadcast approach served as a drive-to-Web catalyst ("Go to www.e-closings.com now and receive . . .") and helped to build a database of leads that could be pursued through telesales and mailings.

Given that E-Closings' founders were hard-core techies, it was surprising that they actually frowned on the inclusion of Web banners in the ad campaign. This was based on their "knowledge" that banner ads' click-through rate (the number of people who actually double-click on an ad so they can be taken to a specific website) is generally low, meaning they often fail to lead site visitors and/or Web surfers to the intended message or the advertiser's site.

But the Extreme Marketers battled this on an important premise: When a form of marketing is said to *suck*, the winners in the business world find a creative way to buck the trend and to turn dross into gold. This is critical to understanding a point that we have made throughout: **Good marketing is good business in microcosm.**

When Sam Walton opened his first Wal-Mart store in "Nowheresville," Arkansas, he was told that the town was too small to support a large discount retailer. (The conventional wisdom had always been "Small towns, small stores." Had Walton prayed at the altar of accepted "wisdom," he would have turned his back on an ingenious idea that made him the richest man in the world. In effect, Walton found a way to create a new kind of discount store that succeeded in the small-town environment (one that featured friendly service and everyday low prices).

As we talked about in the last chapter, to transition from marketing that sucks to marketing that builds business, management must be consistently creative and willing to challenge on all fronts accepted norms—such as "banner advertising never works well."

This book is not a blueprint for spending more money —it is a guide for spending it more effectively to grow companies. In fact, it often reduces marketing budgets and always generates greater sales. That is its essence, its central tenet *AND ITS KEY TO SUCCESS*. It is a formula, an approach, a mind-set, a methodology that every business owner/manager can and should follow.

Newsletters and E-Letters

E-Closings was establishing more than a new company or service—it was introducing an innovative methodology to a hidebound industry, an industry that had resisted dramatic change and still functioned in an outdated manner.

Experience tells us that this set of circumstances requires a compelling introduction of the new concept and, equally important, consistent follow-through on the value proposition. The best course of action is to demonstrate to prospective customers the pragmatic benefits of transitioning from handling certain kinds of real-estate transactions with the current call/fax/paper-trail confusion to E-Closings' central, online environment.

From management's perspective, this would best be accomplished through the publication of a newsletter that would be mailed (and e-mailed) to prospects and referral sources. The idea had merit—and would likely deliver some value—but was ultimately rejected as a costly, time-consuming initiative that the new company would be wise to do without.

This decision reflected a key principle (but one that is often overlooked) of successful marketing: **In all cases, less is more.**

Simply because a marketing tool or program will deliver value does not mean it should be moved beyond the idea stage. Every potential tactic must be viewed in the context of the overall plan and the available budget.

These requirements force management to ask such important questions as:

► Will the marketing tool or initiative simply
   replicate another part of the program?

- Should the dollars be allocated to something else?
- Should we shrink the estimated budget?
- Do we have the talent to do the job exceptionally well?

The hardest part of marketing may very well be rejecting good ideas in order to focus on the sweet spots that will produce more significant returns.

Direct Mail

The idea for an E-Closings newsletter did lead to the creation of a valuable asset. A database originally developed so that E-Closings would know to whom to send its newsletter was used instead as the target list for a direct-mail campaign designed to recruit charter customers and to build the customer base.

Instead of sending the prospects a single piece of communication, which is rarely enough to initiate relationships, the marketers opted for a multistage drip campaign that called for prospects to receive a personalized introduction letter offering a "charter customer" premium, a follow-up postcard focused on the service's key benefits, a direct-response brochure and drive-to-Web card, and a telesales call.

This established a cumulative impact that built a strong case for transitioning to E-Closings.

Print and E-Collateral

E-Closings required three types of print collateral to illustrate (in text and graphics) the company's process and to clearly define its value proposition, as well as to support the execution of the various components of the marketing program.

1. **Main capabilities brochure.** This is the one marketing tool that clearly explains what the company does and how it does it. In the case of E-Closings, the brochure heralded the introduction of a revolutionary means of consummating certain real-estate transactions, and demonstrated the benefits E-Closings delivers to each key customer segment: buyers and sellers, lawyers, title companies, and mortgage bankers. This prestige piece is important for opening doors and consummating transactions with premier organizations.

2. **Direct-response brochures.** This is a scaled-down version of the capabilities brochure designed primarily to generate leads and facilitate the sales cycle.

3. **Drive-to-Web pieces.** These are tools designed to sufficiently pique the curiosity of the prospect to visit the E-Closings website. They served as "teasers" that ended with, "To learn more, visit www.e-closings.com."

All of the collateral pieces were created with a strong call to action ("If you act now, you will receive . . .") and a print or electronic business-reply card.

Once the campaign was constructed, the financial half of the founding entrepreneurial team offered high—if unique—praise.

Shaking his head up and down in agreement with his partner, who had already signed off on the plan, he said, "This is the first time we have been in total agreement that something is a good idea since we decided to become business partners."

The Extreme Marketing plan also required management to ask a number of questions in different categories— on a regular basis—to generate maximum results from the marketing program, whatever the competition did or did not do.

Website

- ► Is our website design up-to-date?
- ► Does our website design reflect our overall corporate branding?
- ► Is our website registered with the appropriate search engines?
- ► Are we analyzing who is visiting the site?
- ► Do we know how many visitors our site attracts?

- Do we know which areas of our site are most popular?
- Do we know which areas of our site are least popular?
- Do we have a "drive-to-Web" campaign to integrate our other marketing material and increase Web traffic?
- Are we updating our site's content weekly? Monthly? Quarterly? Annually?
- Does our site provide visitors with a compelling view of our company's value proposition, products, and services?

E-Commerce

- Is our website simply an online brochure, or is it equipped to conduct transactions online?
- Is sufficient security in place?
- Have we identified which of our products and/or services can be sold directly via the Internet?
- Should we create a new set of products or services that can be sold this way?
- Will we gain competitive advantage by being the first mover in this market?
- Do we have the sufficient functionality behind the site to enable visitors to truly interact with our business?

Database Management

- ► Do we maintain a complete database of our customers/clients?
- ► Is it up-to-date?
- ► Do we enter the names of prospects regularly?
- ► Is the database organized by categories appropriate for existing business and for cross-selling?

The purpose of checklist is clear: Just because you start your Extreme Marketing plan with a blank piece of paper doesn't mean you want to end it that way. You want to have a mechanism in place to capture everything that you are doing right and wrong—and an ongoing plan for improving it.

7. Ready, aim, fire!

Why it beats ready, fire, aim every time ... how to test, execute, and monitor your marketing

PROBLEM

You consistently spend too much money before you discover that all, or some, of your marketing initiatives are delivering poor results.

SOLUTION

Extensively test various approaches before you launch an initiative, in order to discover the ones that will produce the highest return on your marketing investment.

BENEFIT

You will minimize your losses and maximize your gains.

RULE

Sometimes clichés become clichés because they contain a truth worth repeating. One example? Measure twice, cut once.

The only smart way to conduct marketing—more to the point, the only smart way to grow a business—is to approach it this way: Ready, aim, fire. Or to put it more pragmatically:

1. Test
2. Execute
3. Monitor

And then once you have this iterative process down, start again:

1. Test
2. Execute
3. Monitor

Here's how it works.

Taking the real-world test

Pod Productions creates and produces interactive games. Senior management, especially those in marketing, believe that the best way to promote Pod's new *Killer Stalker* CD is to advertise the product on MTV and ESPN. Given a supercool medium—interactive video games—those two outlets offer the ideal demographics. The people who watch MTV and ESPN are the highest per capita consumers of interactive video entertainment.

All the planets appear to be aligned, favoring a major campaign. The price tag: $550,000 to shoot the commercial; another $5 million to run it on air.

But before Pod presses the "go" button, its management team needs to flash back to the legion of high-tech companies that, until the economy sagged, were flinging millions at television advertising in what turned out to be the last-rites rain dance of a dying breed of ready-fire-aim executives. These short-lived firms never tested anything—not their business plans or their so-called services, much less their marketing—convinced that either:

a. They had to move quickly, or they would lose a major opportunity.
b. They didn't need to test anything. Their "golden gut" would tell them ahead of time what would work and what wouldn't.

The executives lost their companies; their shareholders lost a fortune.

So what are we saying when we stress that you should test carefully before you fire? Are we saying that you should contemplate everything for so long that you trade in your business stripes for a tenured position at a hide-bound think tank? Of course not. But on the continuum of decision-making, there is a wide gap between blink-speed and glacial-speed.

A wiser, safer approach is to avoid the extremes and base your decision on empirical evidence.

This brings us to "the Test."

Before Pod, or any business for that matter, commits to a costly marketing campaign, it needs to conduct tests that will indicate, to a reasonable extent, that the company's marketing assumptions will be scoring bull's-eyes in the real world.

You can do this by conducting focus groups with your target audience—but I don't recommend it. The problem I have found with focus groups is that they are never going to tell you something that you don't already know. First of all, the focus group is invariably dominated by one person with a big mouth, and an ego to match, who influences everyone else, despite the best attempts of the moderator.

And even if you conduct multiple focus groups, to try to get a sample reaction that is statistically valid, it doesn't help you much. I remember when we did multiple focus groups throughout the Midwest for American Express. It had bought IDS, the financial-planning company, a few years before and had changed its name to American Express Financial Advisors, but business wasn't as brisk as the company would have liked when it came to marketing to the best prospects: small-business owners. The focus groups were intended to find out why.

Going into the focus groups, we knew that some small business owners thought American Express offering financial advice made sense, and others didn't; a certain number of those prospects knew that American Express offered financial advice, and most didn't; and that most small-business owners had doubts that a large company like American Express would truly understand their needs.

And what did the focus groups tell us?

Some prospects thought American Express offering financial advice made sense, and others didn't.

A certain number of people knew that American Express offered financial advice, and most didn't.

Most small-business owners had doubts that a large company like American Express would truly understand their needs.

Great. We dragged our butts across the country spending millions to "discover" something that we already knew. Remember our image of throwing thousand-dollar bills out the window and calling it marketing? This was it in action. A classic example of Lazy ("it sucks") Marketing.

So why then do marketers use focus groups? I think it is only the ones who are not confident in their own abilities who do. That way, if the product or campaign fails, they can always say, "But the focus groups told us it would be a hit." The focus-group data is a way for them to cover their backsides should something go wrong. These "marketers" have no guts. No instincts. Just a flair for wasting money.

Given that, I don't have much confidence in focus groups. I suggest that you try out your message in a less-expensive medium. In Pod's case, that would mean direct mail, or e-mail marketing to a control group, instead of immediately spending money on television advertising.

No, a printed piece or e-mail won't capture all the glitz and glamour of a television ad. But with creativity and frequency, the return on your marketing investment may be higher.

If the tests indicate that TV is, in fact, the best buy, produce the commercial but hedge your risk by limiting initial placement to "spot TV," where you run a limited number of commercials (spots) within a specific market. Instead of having your ad appear during the first commercial break in MTV's *The Real World*, where the commercials run in every market in the country, maybe you buy time only during the third break, where spots appear just in local markets, and you buy time exclusively in St. Louis and Denver.

Only after you are certain that the ad is producing results do you expand the program to the full campaign.

Another advantage of this approach is that you can test different aspects of your message at the same time, to determine which one is most appealing to potential customers.

For example, recently a leading mutual-fund company was wondering what would be the best way to promote its money-market fund. Was it the power of its brand name? Great customer service? The fact that the firm was one of the most experienced in the industry?

All those things are good, of course, but a company or a product should stand for an overriding value proposition in the consumer's mind; otherwise, the message gets muddy and the consumer becomes confused. The company needed to find the one idea that worked best.

Management tested different messages ("We have award-winning customer service" and "We are one of the oldest and most respected firms in the industry") in different markets, and then ran the most promising ones regionally, so that they could compare them head-to-head.

During this ready-aim-fire phase, the company discovered that every time it said, "We have the highest-yielding money market fund in the nation," the money flowed in. As a result, the company made sure its money-market fund would have the highest yield, even if it was only one basis point (0.01 percent) more than anyone else's.

And once people became investors, the company would try to also sell them its bond and equity funds; that's where the real money was. (We will discuss cross-selling in the next chapter.) And, obviously, the more money investors had at the firm, the less likely they were to switch to another company.

Execute

Interestingly, the execution of a marketing campaign is often considered the "dull stuff." The real genius, it is thought, comes in the idea creation, the epiphany, and the insight that leads to the overall strategy behind the marketing campaign, whatever it is.

Once the geniuses make their magic, they return to the throne to ponder the next flash of brilliance, passing the torch to the "gremlins" assigned to put the magic into action.

This is another major reason why most marketing sucks. Winning ideas win only if they are executed brilliantly.

Let's go back to the marketing of the *Killer Stalker* CD. Once Pod's creative director envisions the "perfect" commercial, she must hand it off to an inspired director and producer, or the vision will fail to come through on the screen. This is where synergy comes into play. The essential equation is: 1 (creative vision) + 1 (creative execution) = 3 (creative alchemy). And the result of $1 + 1 = 3$ is customers and sales.

The idea is not to execute exactly as the blueprint suggests but, rather, to add another dimension that could never have been imagined by the idea creators. Spike Lee, the talented filmmaker, has also worked his magic on Madison

Avenue, producing compelling television commercials for the likes of Nike and Pepsi. Sure, Lee always has a clever storyboard to work with, but his inspired eye behind the camera—and the driving mix of music, video, and street language that he incorporates into his filmmaking—infuses the productions/commercials with extra dimensions. Execution is not about following a recipe. It is about enhancing it.

If we take "execution" outside of the creative/marketing realm, we can see another example of its ability to provide the winning edge. For years, U.S. automakers focused exclusively on design, producing beautiful steel chariots that drove consumers to engage in an annual rite of fashion-based consumption. But when their Japanese competitors decided to shift their focus from design bells and whistles to the long-overlooked arena of "execution," their factories produced a level of quality never before experienced, and the balance of power (and the market share that went with it) shifted to Tokyo. Detroit lost a generation of consumers, many of whom would never considering purchasing an American-made car.

The key point for the Pod Productions of the world—along with every company, large or small, public or private, that sells business-to-business, business-to-consumer, or business-to-nonprofit—is that each element of the marketing process must be executed with imagination and monomaniacal attention to the details. The marketing plan can be fine at the forty-thousand-foot level, but executing and massaging the different elements on the ground, where the rubber hits the road, makes all the difference.

Here's another example of that. We were hired to do marketing for an upscale women's-clothing-store chain. And one of the tactics in the marketing plan called for doing direct-mail letters to affluent households located near the stores. Absolutely the right thing to do.

But in our execution of the idea, we took it a step further: We secured the names of women within a thirty-mile radius of the stores who subscribed to numerous fashion magazines and went after them first. If you subscribe to four fashion magazines, you are probably a "fashion addict" and the absolutely perfect customer for our client.

The more you can target your message the better, and the execution phase is the right place to do that.

Paying attention to execution will also help you avoid these mistakes that lead to *spending that is camouflaged as marketing*:

• Direct-mail letters addressed with mailing labels. The labels scream *junk mail!*

• Brochures written and designed to play it safe (they say nothing edgy, provocative, "out there"). Ironically, playing it safe is perhaps the riskiest strategy you can follow,

Does your **marketing** suck?

since it virtually guarantees that what you have written will not move people to act, to buy, to change their consumption patterns, to try novel services and products (such as *Killer Stalker*). At my company, MSCO, we produced a brochure that is mailed in a neon-green envelope. On the outside of the envelope, in big, bold type we put: **We have a question for you.** Then, on the inside front page, we ask the question: **Does your marketing suck?**

Before producing this, we debated it internally. Would clients and prospects be insulted? Would they think the message was crass? Would we appear to be a firm devoid of the character that companies look for in their marketing firms? All the weight of tradition said, "Don't do it!" but we bit the bullet and proceeded, knowing that we needed to live by a universal rule of effective marketing: **"If it won't make an impact, don't invest in it!"** Fortunately, the rule has paid off. Clients and prospects love the bold, go-for-it tone that drives right to the heart of the issue and makes them think about their current approach to the marketplace. Related to this, when we engage in direct-mail campaigns and then follow up with telephone calls (a must, as we will talk about in a minute!), the prospect often says, "I don't recall receiving your material." But when we respond, "It was the brochure that asked '**Does your marketing suck?**'" virtually everyone says, "Oh yes, I remember now." Bingo! That's what marketing must do.

• **Websites that are brochures in disguise.** Attractive as they may be, they do not make use of the Internet. You cannot connect with the site, engage in interactive inquiries, order things, speak to people, pierce the skin of the business, or benefit from its products and services. If your website is nothing more than an electronic brochure, you are squandering the power of the medium.

Monitor

Okay, so you have come up with a creative concept, and you have tested it, rolled it out, and executed it with extraordinary finesse; now you are ready to reap the rewards (leads/sales/profits) of a marketing tour de force.

Or are you?

All too often, all the pieces appear to be in place—and yet the results fall short of the mark. Compounding the problem, the marketers don't realize that fact until it is too late (i.e., until they have wasted a lot of money), because they fail to monitor the results of the campaign in all but the most superficial, time-delayed ways. Call this Marketing Sucks, Part 2.

Great marketing requires that you be all over the results of the campaign, measuring response rates by raw numbers, percentages of the target group, sales volume, market share, and other revealing benchmarks. And you have to monitor this by the day, the hour, even the minute (in cases where responses can be measured via phone calls or website hits). You need to understand every variable that can impact results and what you can do to raise the bar in your favor. If something works, you want to do more of it, and do it as quickly as possible.

Here are some good ways to obtain the information you need.

Five smart ways to monitor results

1. Ask telemarketers if prospects appear more eager to buy, or are more interested in the pitch, at certain times of the day.

This may lead you to shift the advertising that generates those calls to those peak-response hours. Now, to discover this kind of information, your telemarketers can't be automatons, as is too often the case. And they can't be people whose goal is to make X number of calls during a shift and go home, unfazed by whether or not the calls produced results. The woman we have hired for our telemarketing at MSCO is a former journalist. Not only does she know how to talk to people, but she knows how to ferret out information. For example, if someone says no, she makes a follow-up call to learn why he is rejecting the offer. Of course, not everyone uses telemarketing—and it is often impractical if you are trying to reach millions of people to sell something with a low profit margin—but I would argue that more companies should. They don't need to hire telemarketing firms—they can use their existing sales force. If each salesperson made just ten telemarketing calls a day, he would reach more than 2,500 people during the course of the year, people who could tell you what is, and what is not, right about your product offering. (And you would increase revenue in the process.)

2. Look beyond the number of website hits to the quality of the hits.

This can be accomplished by analyzing the ratio of hits to orders or leads produced by the hits. It may turn out that your most active visitation periods are the least productive in terms of business-building opportunities. If so, that means something has to change. Maybe your message. Your first marketing campaign will give you a baseline. Even if only one person in a thousand (0.001 percent) responds, you have something to compare your second effort to.

3. Measure lead/sales volume before and after advertising appears.

In addition, use this process to determine the point of diminishing returns from a creative approach, publication, Web portal, or broadcast media. Make a change at the first sign of a weakening trend.

4. Ask your sales channel (retailers/distributors/customers) if your marketing has:

a. Prompted them to buy your product/services. You can double-check by providing different phone numbers, or different websites for customers to respond to, in each of your advertisements placed in different distribution channels. That way, you will have a solid handle on where your sales are coming from.

b. Driven them to make incremental purchases of your product/service.

c. Discouraged them from switching to a competitor's products/services.

5. See if your competitors are beginning to imitate your approach.

This is often a sign that you are getting results. Your competitors are more likely to copy you if your marketing efforts are hurting them.

Clearly, monitoring provides you with important information on the success and/or failure of your marketing campaign. But its real power comes as a critical component of our three-part process: Test. Measure. Monitor.

With the knowledge about response rates and trends in hand, you have a benchmark against which you can—*you must*—restart and enrich the process, testing new approaches, new markets, new demographics, new messages, constantly seeking to produce a higher return on your marketing investment. Change one variable—say, try handwritten addresses on the envelopes versus typed ones—hold everything else constant, and measure what happens.

Case in point: Herb Vest, founder of Dallas-based H. D. Vest Financial Services, whom we talked about in Chapter 4.

When Vest came up with his idea to license his fellow accountants to sell, and profit from, the investment and insurance products they had traditionally referred to others (stockbrokers/insurance agents), he needed a way to sell those accountants on his idea.

Vest wrote a folksy direct-mail letter, inviting his peers to get licensed with his nascent company. Direct-marketing gurus would laugh at the letter—and indeed, my first reaction when I saw it was that he needed something that was more sophisticated to appeal to financial professionals like accountants—but Vest believed in what he had written and used it as his primary recruitment tool.

However—and this is a big, unusual however—Vest continued to test new versions of the letter written by consultants, his management team, and professional copywriters. Although nothing performed better than the original, the testing led Vest to fine-tune the document and the way it is presented (types of paper, envelope size, and use of colors).

Over time, Vest outgunned and outfoxed the giant financial-services firms (all of whom gravitated to the

CPA market he discovered), recruiting more than nine thousand accountants thanks to the power of his direct-mail concept (continually tested, executed, monitored—over and over again). He kept testing his pitch letter until the day he sold the company for $127 million.

It ain't sexy—but it *is* profitable

As we can see, a major component of Extreme Marketing is to develop a plan and stay micro-focused on it. Yes, monitoring, measuring, and the other blocking and tackling fundamentals are not as compelling or inspirational as the creative process, but they provide the business discipline that helps to assure a significant return on investment. And they provide checks and balances to help make certain that your company fails to produce sloppy marketing that sucks.

8. Pick the low-hanging fruit

Why you don't have to spend a fortune to boost sales and earnings

PROBLEM

You have limited marketing dollars, yet you need a substantial boost to your sales and earnings.

SOLUTION

Pick the low-hanging fruit, such as selling more to people who already have a relationship with you.

BENEFIT

You should get a whopping return on your marketing investment.

RULE

While you are seeking to open entirely new markets, or sell new products, remember that there is low-hanging fruit all around you ready to be picked. Cultivate this first.

I magine this scenario: An aggressive, highly regarded chain of home-improvement stores negotiates with a hot fashion designer to have him develop a licensed line of high-fashion paints, wallpaper, and window treatments. After the deal is inked, and the stores are stocked with the attractive and highly salable goods, management hangs black drapes over all of the shelves designed to display the merchandise. The result? Consumers cannot see that the chain offers an incredibly attractive line of home goods.

Far-fetched? Not as much as you may think. The failure to clearly inform customers and clients of the products and services that companies have for sale is widespread throughout virtually every industry.

An informal roundtable held by a Hartford, Connecticut–based consulting firm demonstrated this (much to the pain and chagrin of the firm's managing partner). One evening, a group of clients were invited to spend an hour with the firm's management to talk about how well the firm served them. (That, in and of itself, was a terrific idea, one that more companies should emulate. Periodically, take clients out for a nice dinner. Reserve a room at a fine restaurant, and use your guests as a sounding board.)

At one point in the roundtable discussion, the managing partner asked if the clients were pleased with his firm's services. Although the overwhelming majority said that they were indeed happy with the firm, and more than satisfied with its performance on their behalf, most were united in a single but highly important complaint. They made it clear that the firm failed to inform them of the full suite of its services. As one client put it bluntly, "You don't tell us what you do!"

Although the firm offered a broad range of services, the partners in charge of client accounts tended to focus only on their area of expertise, keeping their clients in the dark about the broader range of the firm's capabilities. Clearly, this was the near equivalent of acquiring a designer line of furnishings and putting black drapes over the shelves.

Specifically:

• One of the clients who complained had turned a children's-crafts business from a start-up into a $50 million a year enterprise. When she went through a highly contentious divorce, it became necessary to engage a professional to conduct an appraisal of her business. This would be important in negotiating the divorce settlement. At this emotional time in her life, she would have liked nothing more than to work with the Hartford consulting firm that she trusted as her ally in business, a resource that had helped her business grow. But she turned elsewhere, because she didn't know that the firm offered valuation services. All too often while companies are looking for the "big win," they are engaging in the "big loss." Here, simply because the client was not informed of the full range of services, she was forced to go outside her comfort range to an unfamiliar service provider, and the consulting firm lost the potential revenue of a business-valuation engagement.

- Another client who owned a chain of automobile dealerships shared a similar story. He had founded the business with his brother, who—until his recent death—had managed the operations side of the business, while the survivor had focused on sales. At the time of the brother's death, the business needed to upgrade its information-technology systems. Unfamiliar and uncomfortable with technology applications, the surviving brother turned to a technology firm to assess the dealership's existing systems, recommend an updated network, and install the related hardware and software. The sin of omission was that the Hartford-based consulting firm offered information-technology services but had failed to make this known to a sufficient segment of its client base. Once again, a long-standing client was forced to come out of his comfort zone and go elsewhere for a service that the firm offered. Another example of the firm's missing the opportunity to pick low-hanging fruit.

We are going to explore the importance of cross-selling in a second. But first, an important point. Cross-selling is not the only form of picking low-hanging fruit.

Obviously:

- ► You could find a competitor with a higher price and undercut him. This is especially effective if you are both selling a commodity. And it works particularly well as a "Trojan horse." You use the low price to lure customers into your store (or into visiting your website), where, you hope, they will find higher-priced merchandise to buy.
- ► You can add a feature that no one else has. There are three dry cleaners in your town? How much market share could you gain if you offered to pick up and deliver? Seems simplistic? So what: It works. When I moved to the town I now live in, only one dry cleaner offered pickup and delivery service. Given that my days are crammed—which gives me no time for errands—I selected the one firm that would do the errand for me. (And that company, in turn, picked the low-hanging fruit: my dry-cleaning business.)

► You can identify (and hire away) salespeople at competitors who have relationships with customers you covet. Yes, sometimes they will have "noncompete" contracts with their current employer, but often they won't, and equally often the noncompetes are written so broadly as to be unenforceable.

But while these—and the other variations you could identify—are all appealing options, the biggest opportunity to pick low-hanging fruit exists in cross-selling. So let's focus our attention there.

The importance of cross-selling

Cross-selling is powerful because it is pervasive and relatively easy to transition opportunity to results, measured in dollars and cents.

The vast majority of businesses have a customer base composed of individuals who have purchased their products and services in the past. The disturbing paradox (proof positive that most marketing sucks) on which few businesspeople will challenge you is the fact that "it is easier to sell something to an existing customer than to a prospect who is unfamiliar with your business." However, while conceding it is true, few companies act on this fact. All too often, companies spend virtually all of their marketing dollars, time, and talent seeking to generate new business relationships while the low-hanging fruit dies on the vine.

This is evidenced by the fact that the majority of companies fail to capitalize on the exceptional opportunity represented by their existing customers. Lazy Marketing! Lazy Marketing!

A perfect example is a New England–based furniture company with a house file of twenty-six thousand customers who have purchased sofas, tables, beds, carpets, and accessories from the firm's eight retail stores for more than two decades. This customer universe is diverse in age, gender, income, and personality, but they are united in a predisposition to purchase the furniture company's products. And yet the company does nothing to encourage them to do one of the things that gives them great pleasure in life: visit the stores, buy something beautiful, and make their homes more wonderful environments.

Why don't companies do more cross-selling? There are three primary reasons.

1. They just don't think of it.

Strange but true. They have collected key information about customers—names, addresses, and often phone numbers and e-mail addresses as well—and then they do nothing with it, other than to send out the occasional brochure or circular. That's dumb—and lazy. If you know someone bought a couch from you, why not send her a personalized letter that says, "We just got in an end table that would go perfectly with that sofa you bought from us four months ago. Come in this week, and we'll give you 20 percent off." By simply mailing customers a postcard promoting attractive products in the stores, they would generate significant traffic and sales from this highly qualified pool of loyal patrons. By failing to take this step, these otherwise aggressive merchants are remiss in cross-selling and, thus, in harvesting low-hanging fruit.

2. It's "too pushy."

Who says attempts at cross-selling have to be hard sell? DirecTV knows you bought its NFL Sunday Ticket—a programming option that allows you to watch the televised version of every pro football game, not just the one being beamed into your market. What is so hard sell about DirecTV sending you an e-mail saying, "As someone who bought the NFL Sunday Ticket, you are entitled to a 20 percent discount on the NBA Pass" (which allows you to see every pro basketball game).

3. It's "not professional," or your staff feels uncomfortable doing it.

This is a common objection and gets back to our discussion that you can't turn a nonsalesperson into a salesperson. But that isn't your intention here. You aren't asking a lawyer to take out his order book, or an architect to try to close a sale. You are asking them to listen and then educate clients or customers. Suppose you are a criminal lawyer, and your client mentions in passing that he has succession issues or estate-planning concerns. You can say, right then, "You know, we have someone at the firm who is an expert in . . ." If that is too direct, mention the same thing in a follow-up note to the meeting that you just had with the client.

It doesn't matter what approach you take. What's important is that you do it, and that your people do as well. If they are uncomfortable, offer coaching on the cross-selling educational process. If you think a more tangible motivation is the way to go, do that. The managing partner at one of Chicago's premier law firms told every attorney who worked there that he was going to make them the highest-paid lawyers in the country, but one of the things they had to do to achieve that status was cross-sell legal services offered by their colleagues in the firm.

Cross-selling in action

Making customers aware of product offerings and seeking to cross-sell them with a simple postcard, letter, or brochure is important, but just the start. Consider it Extreme Marketing 101, the price of admission.

Advanced Extreme Marketers take this concept to

sophisticated levels and are rewarded handsomely for it. Let's explore two examples.

The Mitchell family, owners of Richards in Greenwich and Mitchells in Westport, upscale clothing stores in affluent Connecticut towns, have made a science of data-mining its customer base to grow the business to $65 million in annual revenues. Much of this sales volume, which make Richards and Mitchells two of the most successful stores in the nation, is attributed to management's monomaniacal focus on learning as much as possible about its customers on a personal and professional level and then applying this knowledge to service them, building a loyal clientele base. With the customers' assurance of confidentiality, associates at Mitchells and Richards use personal contact and probing questions along with sales SKU data to gather a wealth of information about customers, such as

- Birthdays
- Names of children and spouse
- Birthdays of children and spouse
- Favorite clothing designers
- Favorite colors
- Buying patterns
- Dollar volume of cumulative annual purchases

Unlike other businesses that gather this data and then let it sit idly on a server, Mitchells and Richards apply it in a series of pragmatic initiatives designed to drive customer loyalty and sales.

For example, customers:

- ► Are often called on their birthday, or sent a birthday greeting.
- ► Are given advance notice when their favorite designers' merchandise has arrived.
- ► Receive a "bonus" check each spring for anywhere from $10–$150 based on their cumulative purchases the previous holiday season. This provides an incentive to the best customers to remain loyal to the store and increase their purchases during a regular price period.

The second example involves Pottery Barn, which sells home furnishings and accessories. The company invites customers to fill out an entry form for a gift certificate and drop it in a fishbowl placed at the register.

The form asks for the customer's name, street address, and, most important, e-mail address. For pennies—the price of the pad that contains the form to fill out—this Extreme Marketing technique enables Pottery Barn to cross-sell customers immediately and effectively. I learned this firsthand.

I recently visited the Pottery Barn store in Westport, Connecticut, filled out the entry form, dropped it in the bowl, and went shopping in the store (purchasing, as it turns out, a glass flower vase).

Within a few days, a beautifully constructed graphic e-mail arrived on my laptop screen, enticing me to purchase additional Pottery Barn products, including sale merchandise and new arrivals. Because I could see the goods and almost touch them, Pottery Barn effectively brought the store to me, and tempted a proven customer—one who liked the Pottery Barn concept, aesthetics, and price points—to extend his shopping experience, in this case online.

This Extreme Marketing tactic is interesting for two reasons. Pottery Barn

1. Secures the e-mail addresses for the price of an entry slip.
2. Stays close to its customers with frequent e-mails that entertain, inform, and prompt the customer to shop, shop, and shop.

Proof positive that Extreme Marketing doesn't have to be expensive.

It is often the inexpensive, overlooked steps that, when stitched together and integrated in a cross-selling program, enable a business to cultivate copious amounts of low-hanging fruit.

Companies are often so focused on "what they sell" that they overlook "what they can sell, but fail to." Consider the case of BAJA—a fictitious name for a real company—which specializes in the design and installation of home entertainment and automation systems. In the "love them and leave them" approach that is all too common among companies large and small, BAJA would book a sale, design the customer's technology, and then install it meticulously and professionally.

But once the job was done, BAJA would move on to the next prospect, leaving behind the most recent installation with a satisfied client who had been sold, billed, and put in the company's files.

BAJA's focus on detail and excellence in products and services created an enormous amount of goodwill, which the company could have leveraged in making additional sales. For example, it could have done everything from providing financing for the home entertainment systems—which could easily cost more than $100,000—to providing extended-warranty service. But management rarely cultivated this opportunity. Instead, they turned to the next referral and simply moved on, serving an always-growing list of customers and leaving behind an equally growing volume of satisfied customers.

Extreme Marketers turned this asset into revenues by teaching BAJA to look forward and backward simultaneously. In addition to launching a cross-selling initiative focused on products and systems, the company launched a new program, selling service contracts to customers. This turned a "one-off" business into an "annuity." For as long as BAJA's customers lived in their homes and retained their systems, they would likely pay the service contracts, from which BAJA earned a substantial commission for doing virtually nothing.

The BAJA example should prompt Extreme Marketers to look at every part of their sales continuum to identify opportunities to enrich its customer value proposition and its revenues. For example, consider offering

- ► Customized products and services for higher-margin prices
- ► Accelerated deliveries on made-to-order merchandise for a premium fee
- ► Service contracts
- ► Gift certificates

Gift certificates are particularly interesting for a number of reasons: When customers are pleased with your products and services, they will refer your business to friends and associates. The best way to encourage them to do this is to suggest that they give gift certificates on those occasions where they might otherwise give cash or a specific gift.

When customers give gift certificates to your business, they provide you with two powerful benefits:

• The recipient visits your business, discovers its range of offerings, and is likely to (a) make purchases in excess of the certificate value and (b) become a regular customer in her own right.

- In many cases, gift certificates are cashed in long after they are purchased. This gives your business free use of the funds extended for the purchase of the certificate. Think of it as getting interest-free loans. (This, by the way, is one of the ways American Express makes exceptional profits on the company's traveler's checks.)

A premier senior living community in Westchester County, New York, uses gift certificates as a way of turning its residents into an ancillary sales force. Every resident who encourages a friend to move into the community receives a credit of $500 on his monthly rent. Given that seniors want to have their friends join them at the residences, and that saving $500 per successful referral is a major financial inducement for them, the program is a highly successful Extreme Marketing tactic.

Chances are good that with a bit of thought and imagination, you could develop a similar program for your business. Put your employees to work trying to think of the best ideas, and reward them with paid vacations.

Extreme Marketing means using every legal tactic to achieve your goals. The goal is to get your machine running at the point where the competition stops.

9. Don't go back to the office...yet

Start an Extreme Marketing program by stopping all your marketing until you find out how each part of your program justifies itself in dollars and cents

PROBLEM

There could be a huge amount of slippage between what you've learned here and what gets implemented inside your company.

SOLUTION

Before you go back to work, figure out how you are going to put into effect new programs and procedures based on what you've read in this book. *And halt all marketing programs until you do.*

BENEFIT

By the time you resume your marketing, you will have programs in place that actually justify their keep.

RULE

The first rule of medicine is also the last rule of marketing: Do no harm. Immediately suspend every marketing program you have under way, and stop all new initiatives you have on the drawing board, unless you can *quantitatively* prove they will generate more money than they cost.

The only thing worse than conducting marketing that sucks is to recognize it for what it is—Lazy Marketing—and do little or nothing about it. But this is precisely what you will be tempted to do. Although you may agree with the principles and ideas of Extreme Marketing, once you return to your office—and its normal flow of issues and challenges, opportunities, and problems—you are likely to free-fall into your day-to-day routine and resume business as usual.

That means you will get little or nothing out of what you have read. For this reason, I have a strong suggestion. Once you are done reading, *don't go back to the office!*

No, I am not suggesting that you quit your job or sell your business.

But what I am saying is that instead of charging right back into your work, you should set aside a block of time to think about the issues I have raised and about how you can transition from Lazy Marketing to Extreme Marketing.

I don't mean thinking about this between meetings,

e-mails, and phone calls. I am talking about taking the time to really think. I suggest that this be done on a Sunday morning, locked in your study at home. Or on a park bench. Anywhere you are assured you can have an extended block of time with no interruptions.

And find the time soon. Today. Tomorrow. No matter what, don't let it go beyond a week from today. The longer you wait, the harder it is going to be to change anything.

Once you are assured of this time to think, you'll want to come up with the most efficient way of implementing what you have learned here. The best way to accomplish that is to create a road map that will help you identify the weaknesses in your company's marketing and show you how and when you can address them.

To help you take stock, and to move in the right direction, consider following these steps.

1. Stop every marketing program you have under way that you don't have a legal obligation to continue, unless you can prove that it is producing a substantial return on the money invested in it.

That's right: Stop all marketing, and yes, that includes advertising.

For all of you who think that your business would fall off a cliff if you took this step, let me introduce you to Fox's, a national off-price women's-clothing chain. Fox's has twelve stores, and it had allowed each store manager to determine how and where to advertise his location. What this meant was that people who knew little or nothing about marketing were spending a combined $250,000 of the company's money without rhyme or reason. While some managers advertised their stores in the local papers, others wouldn't dream of spending money that way. You couldn't find common positioning from store to store.

The first thing the owner did, when he decided to implement Extreme Marketing, was to put a moratorium on all advertising spending for three months. He needed that time to determine what he should, and should not, be doing with his company's marketing.

During those three months, sales continued without any noticeable change.

So the first step is, unless you know that the program is currently making you money, stop spending until you have determined what your Extreme Marketing plan is going to look like.

To help you figure it out, take an inventory of all your current marketing initiatives and list them on a sheet of paper or on a computer screen. Include advertising, public relations, brochures, events, direct mail, trade shows, in-store merchandising, newsletters, websites, and everything else.

2. After you have listed each initiative, write down the reason you conduct it.

As you do so, seek to justify the dollars that you spend on these marketing programs.

Now, justification does not mean, "We are a retailer, so, of course, we have to advertise." Justification means you can *prove* that you are making more money from each marketing program you have in place than you are spending on it. If you can, keep the program, for now. Later, when you are done with your analysis, you are going to retain only the programs that generate the highest returns, but for the moment, keep everything that is making you money.

3. Note the marketing initiatives you do not *conduct.*

These may include advertising, public relations, brochures, events, and direct mail. Next to each, write down why you don't do them, seeking to justify your lack of action in this area. Any time you write down an explanation that is nothing more than a traditional marketing rule, challenge it. For example, you have never done direct mail because "everyone knows high-ticket items need to be sold face-to-face." Write yourself a note to test a direct-mail campaign within three months.

Delving deeper

Once you have completed the first three steps, return to the list of initiatives you do conduct, and seek to compute the return on investment you achieve from them.

For example, assume you advertise once a month in the Sunday edition of your local newspaper, and you know that those ads cost you $20,000 per year. How much, exactly, are they bringing in?

(If you don't know what kind of incremental sales volume is generated by your advertising, develop a tracking mechanism. For example, attach a coupon that customers can bring to your business to secure a discount. This way, you will know where at least a significant percentage of leads/customers are coming from. Or you can use a coded telephone system that tracks calls by specific media. This way, you can determine, when a call comes in, if it was generated by a local radio station, a direct-mail letter, a television program, or the Sunday-newspaper ads.)

We are assuming here that you are generating a positive return. Otherwise, as we discussed in the third step, you would have killed the expenditures.

The question becomes: Could you be making more money than you are? To find out, you may want to:

a. Revise the creative strategy of your ads, or other programs, to see if that will improve the return on your marketing investment. Simply because a marketing program doesn't produce a significant return doesn't mean you should throw the baby out with the bathwater. It may be that you need a more powerful message or a different creative approach to get people to respond to and buy your product or service.

b. In the case of your advertising, consider changing from the Sunday edition to the weekday edition. Given your market, and your product or service, perhaps Sunday is the wrong day to advertise. Experimentation is critical to finding the right mix of marketing initiatives and nuances to develop an Extreme Marketing plan that delivers a high yield.

View everything you do with an eye toward making certain that you can conduct a transition from Lazy Marketing to Extreme Marketing. As you have discovered by now, there is a major difference between conducting a checklist of marketing activities—"Let's see, we're advertising on TV and radio, in magazines and through e-mail, so something has gotta work"—and engaging in marketing that is designed to achieve a powerful impact in the marketplace. To make this transition, you must consider the following key factors:

- Is the message powerful and compelling enough to gain the market's attention? How do you know? Are you testing? Constantly?

- Is your offer attractive enough to distinguish you from the competition and to turn prospects into customers or clients? (Do you see your market share climbing as a result of your marketing efforts?)

- Do you engage in creative ways to increase the profile of your company and raise the profile of its competitive advantage?

- Do you do everything possible to wring incremental revenue out of every marketing dollar you spend?

- Are you consistent and persistent in taking your message to the marketplace, as opposed to dabbling in marketing? In other words, ask yourself if your marketing is conducted on an integrated basis—that is, does each of the elements of your marketing reinforce every other? This is the only way to generate the maximum return on your marketing dollars.

You can plot this out graphically by using lines and arrows to show what benefits advertising generates for P.R., and P.R. generates for advertising, and advertising generates for direct mail, for your website.

It's got to tie together

As you look at the integration of your marketing elements graphically, you will come to see more clearly how you must knit them together to generate the kinds of synergies that make $1 + 1 = 3$.

Sometimes truth is stranger than fiction. If you were told that a company would go through the Herculean public-relations effort of getting its product featured on a global cable network linked to a dot-com destination, only to have the consumer be unable to purchase the product promoted, you would think that that would be impossible. But Lazy Marketing strikes every day and hurts companies.

So we return to our caveat: *Don't go back to the office . . . yet.* Not until you have determined to engage in marketing only for the sake of growing your business—not for the sake of marketing—and that you will do everything you can to make certain that the initiatives you launch are structured to achieve maximum impact in the marketplace.

You are not in the process of marketing to protect your butt, or satisfy your ego, or demonstrate that you're a well-rounded businessperson. ("Hey look, Ma, I'm marketing.") At the end of the day, your marketing must generate more money than it costs. If your marketing does that, you will increase revenues and profits and, therefore, the ultimate valuation of your business.

Put all this to work—now!

All too often, businesspeople go to seminars in hotels, training centers, and universities, and spend all kinds of money learning all kinds of things and getting hyped up about the kinds of changes they need to make to help their businesses become more successful.

All that learning, and all that hype, and all that motivation, and all that energy and zeal often float out the window as soon as they go back to work and get lost in the usual treadmill of answering phone calls and e-mails, going to meetings, having conversations, putting out fires, and searching for opportunities.

However, this cannot be an excuse.

Extreme Marketing is just that: extreme. It requires a determination to take things to the max in every way and to make certain that there are no exceptions.

That is a key difference between companies that grow in size and profitability and market share and power and clout, and those that don't. And there is no reason your company cannot be one of the firms that soar.

Whether you are successful at this point or not, or whether you have grown to this point, or want to grow bigger, doesn't make a difference. The fact is that every company must either consistently move ahead or, inevitably, fall behind. There is no staying in place.

Companies that fail to strive for growth inevitably fall behind, shrink, and ultimately die. This is your choice, and no internal tinkering will help you grow the business significantly. Yes, it may increase profitability (by reducing overhead) and improve customer service and make your company a nicer place to work, and all that is fine. But remember Tom Watson's enormously important observation: "Nothing happens until someone sells something."

If you wait to go back to the office until that thought settles in your mind, and until you have decided that you will take drastic action to make certain that the concept permeates your culture and everything you do in your business, then you will make the transition from a Lazy Marketer to being an Extreme Marketer, and you will reap the benefits that come from that dramatic change.

Conclusion:
Good luck
The nuts and bolts of one real-world plan

I sent the following to a retailer that wanted to hire us to do a short-term public-relations campaign for them.

As we talked about in Chapter 5, there is no such thing as a one-trick pony. You can't employ one tactic—in this case public relations—and then check off "marketing" on your "to do" list. It just doesn't work that way in the real world.

As you will see, we offered a different solution.

Great companies recognize the need to be viewed as more than the sum of their parts.

This is what effective marketing is all about. Beyond logos, tag lines, naming conventions, public relations, and advertising, it is <u>all about making certain that a business is perceived in a</u> <u>compelling manner that provides a powerful competitive</u> <u>advantage and an overwhelming motivation to purchase its</u> <u>products and services.</u>

Mary Smith's (a fictitious name for a real company) has not yet achieved this position. An upscale suburban New York home furnishings firm, it is a successful company with a sound business model and a strong, scalable retail format (as reflected in its Outlet Stores), but it lacks the "more than the sum of its parts" quality that drove the growth of Bloomingdale's, Neiman Marcus, Polo, and countless other well-branded retail environments.

In fact, Mary Smith's has a "half brand," one that is not fully developed and is often confusing. (Who is Mary? What is the outlet?) And it's a (half) brand that does not radiate the kind of power that builds sufficient traffic, loyalty, excitement, and distinction to grow into a regional and national powerhouse.

Interestingly, all of the elements are in place: They are simply not integrated and leveraged to achieve the goal of greatness.

The time has come to take this step through the development of a carefully planned and meticulously orchestrated marketing campaign designed to accomplish the following key objectives:

- Create magic and meaning behind the Mary Smith's name
- Turn the name into a real brand, with the depth and excitement to drive the company's growth
- Develop an unquestionable competitive advantage
- Substantially increase the customer base and repeat purchases from current customers
- Accelerate store traffic, and increase the average gross sale

- Gain a higher return on advertising investments
- Enhance the business model in preparation for regional/national expansion.

MSCO views effective public relations as far more than a series of print and broadcast placements. Unless this coverage is set in the context of a traffic-building/loyalty-building/brand-building plan, it is little more than a Band-Aid process that provides only short-term benefits. Our recommendation is to move well beyond the standard P.R. campaign to an integrated media/merchandising/event campaign that, yes, builds traffic and sales, but more important, also builds a powerful brand that provides the momentum to turn a good company into a great one.

ACTION PLAN

MARCH Bring the woman behind the brand name—Mary Smith—*to life,* through a series of promotions establishing the company's heritage as rooted in art and design as opposed to traditional retailing. Mary Smith's success as an artist is not well known outside her suburban hometown. <u>We must establish Mary as an artist and designer whose vision gave birth to the business and is woven through its products/services/culture.</u>

MSCO will package the Mary story in a way that uses the legacy of her artistic achievements to add depth and resonance to the brand and drive traffic to the stores. Our press work will focus most intensely on Mary's artistic/design vision, as opposed to the human-interest angle of "local woman makes good."

As a key part of this strategy, we will work with a museum to host a retrospective of Mary's modern work. The museum event would be launched with a black-tie reception honoring Mary and attended by important figures in the arts and design community. We will also create *The Mary Smith Vision* mini-brochures for in-store distribution and host in-store extensions of the retrospective at each of the stores, conducted as informal receptions honoring Mary.

APRIL Build on the momentum of the Mary-as-an-artist/designer legacy by launching a major promotion of the company's interior-design services/prowess. The goals are to:

- Distinguish Mary Smith's from furniture stores that simply move furniture from the showroom to the home, without vision, insight, or guidance.
- Demonstrate that inspired design is not the exclusive purview of the Mario Buatta/Park Avenue social set. We will get across the point that talented designers, imbued with the Mary Smith's vision, are available at every one of the company's stores and provide their services to customers free of charge.
- Illustrate the results that can be achieved when a Mary

Smith's designer works with you to create an exceptional home.

This will be accomplished through the following initiatives:

- Host designer workshops in all Mary Smith's stores, moving to a different room each week: bedroom, living room, dining room, children's room.
- Base all advertising on the design service/workshops theme.
- Engage in extensive public relations to introduce the designer services, explain the process of working with an in-store designer, demonstrate the wonderful results (before and after stories), and provide design tips and philosophies.
- Distribute a Mary Smith's designer services mini-brochure in-store, through customer and prospect mailings, and to the media.
- Invite the public (through advertising) to bring in photos of rooms they would like redesigned, for complimentary in-store makeover suggestions/consultations with Mary Smith's designers.
- Invite print and broadcast media—including local press, shelter magazines, lifestyle TV, and radio—to cover the workshop.
- Publicize people whose homes have been designed by Mary Smith's.

- Build a design component into the website, and drive visitors to the site through the advertising/PR/workshops.

MAY Launch a series of in-store promotions, workshops, seminars, and demonstrations—backed by advertising, P.R., and the new Mary Smith's brochure we will create—focused on a different classification each week: rugs, antiques, accessories, pine. Using rugs as an example, we will reinforce the Mary Smith's designer/vision branding by securing media placements and in-store promotions on such topics as:

- What is a true Oriental rug?
- Should you buy new or antique?
- Why should you build your room around a rug?
- What makes a quality rug?
- Which regions of the world make the best rugs?
- How can you select the best rugs for your home?

We will engage in similar initiatives for each of the classifications (antiques, accessories, etc.).

JUNE Launch "Discover Tuscany at Mary Smith's." This will kick off with a major event that will transform Mary Smith's Outlet Stores into a virtual Tuscany, complete with presentations on the furniture, food, and lifestyle of this romantic region. To add media firepower to the event, we will seek a major figure associated with Tuscany.

We will seek to replicate the kind of magical events that Bloomingdale's conducted so masterfully in the Marvin Traub era. Consider Bloomies' late-1970s India event (which I chronicled in *Like No Other Store in the World*):

> *Behind-the-scenes activities progressed in New York. Much of this centered around the eleventh floor, at 59th Street, where Barbara D'Arcy laid the plans for in-store decorative devices to convey the taste and feel of India. Silk ornaments, gauze wall hangings, vivid temple paintings, tents and ornamental costumes were designed and produced. For external publicity, a series of special India ads were produced for newspapers and the May issue of* Vogue *(the magazine made India the theme of that issue). In addition, Bloomingdale's arranged for a black-tie in-store dinner, a press conference, and a week of Indian Festivals of Lights, Music and Food.*

MSCO will seek to bring Tuscany-related partners (including distributors) into the event and include indigenous food, bottled water, clothing, and art.

JULY AND AUGUST Engage in mix of P.R. themes suited for the summer months:

- Design ideas for summer living
- Mary Smith's licensing business
- Accessories service/makeovers
- A VIP party/sale at the warehouse for the real-estate brokerage community
- Summer sales
- Features extolling the virtues of the Outlet experience (and, in turn, delineating the two components of the brand, Premium and Outlet)
- Antique shopping (popular in the summer)
- Window treatments
- Fabrics

SEPTEMBER AND OCTOBER If the campaign continues, we suggest a series of events—all led by related P.R. and in-store promotions—focused on the Outlet design themes: Countryside, Bombay, Children, and Mozambique.

Additional thoughts:

- We will need to develop a comprehensive press kit developing key themes, including the company's founder, its design/art roots, its vision, its designer services, its classifications, its management, and its licensing. All will be captured in backgrounders, bios, vision statements, and corporate philosophy.
- All promotions will need to be featured on the website.
- We should develop a monthly postcard mailing to cus-

tomers, local media, and shelter magazines (with tests to prospects), reinforcing all themes and events cited in the Action Plan.

- Customers should be provided with passwords to enter a "special finds" section of the website.
- All stores will have guest books and design portfolios.
- The company's database will be refined and used to continuously data-mine for customer-centric marketing.

This had a happy ending. Mary Smith's sales and earnings substantially exceeded the cost of the marketing initiatives. And that, after all, is why you market in the first place.

B

C

focus groups, 172–74
Forbes (magazine), 29
Ford, Bill, 129–30
Ford Motor Co., 38, 130
Fox's (off-price clothing
  chain), 205–6

G

Gates, Bill, 100, 101, 137
Gerstner, Lou, 106–8, 133
gift certificates, 197,
  200–201
Good Housekeeping Seal of
  Approval, 97
growth, business, 11, 16, 17,
  28, 60–67, 141, 211
Guardian Life, 52
guest books, 223
gullibility, 131–32

H

hard sell, 194
H. D. Vest Financial Services,
  116–18, 185–86
HealthTech (fictitious
  technology firm), 88–89,
  91

hope, sales approach and,
  78–80

I

IBM, 27–28, 50, 106–8, 112,
  133, 137
imagination, 112
  knowledge vs., 90
imitation, competitor, 184
impact
  brochures with, 178–79
  marketing with, 209–10,
  211
infomercials, 29–30,
  94–100
innovation, 26, 27, 43, 112,
  137, 155
in-store merchandising, 206,
  220
integrated marketing, 42, 43,
  132, 210
  for online real-estate
  transaction service,
  144–68
  for suburban home-
  furnishings firm,
  215–23
  as synergy, 68, 121–41,
  144, 211

interactive video games, 170–71, 176, 179

Internet. *See* e-commerce; e-mail marketing; websites

investment return, 11, 14, 30–31, 43, 99, 115–16, 186, 208–9

J

Jobs, Steve, 100

junk bonds, 101–2

junk mail, 57, 178

K

Kforce.com, 124

Killer Stalker (interactive video game), 171, 176, 179

knowledge, imagination vs., 90

L

law-firm marketing, 65–75, 194–95

Lazy Marketing, 40–42, 108, 193

accountants and, 53–59, 118

focus groups and, 173–74

mistakes checklist, 126–28

professional-services firms and, 67

transition to Extreme Marketing, 204–13

leadership, 128–41

Lee, Spike, 176–77

less-is-more principle, 163–64

life-insurance companies, 77–81

Lillian August (furniture chain), 25–26

logistics monitoring, 133–36

logos, 152, 215

loyalty, customer, 196–97, 217

M

made-to-order merchandise, 200

mailing labels, 57, 178

management consulting, 137

in real-estate firm's
campaign, 147,
153–68
purchase patterns, 90

R

radio advertising, 208
Ralph Lauren, 69
Real Estate News, 147
real-estate online transaction
firm, 144–68
results measurement,
133–36, 182–84
revenue growth, 11, 19, 90,
119
Richards (clothing store),
196–97
risk acceptance, 112

S

sales, 49–86
educating as factor in,
70–71, 194–95
Executive Briefings and,
70–71
training in, 66–67, 76, 80,
194–95

volume tracking 23, 51,
159, 183, 208
salespeople
closers vs. schmoozers, 76,
83, 84
hiring away of
competitor's, 192
longevity vs. effectiveness
of, 85–86
Salomon Smith Barney,
32–37, 44
schmoozing, 76, 80, 83, 84,
99
Schwab, Charles, 137
seminars, business, 212
senior living community,
82–85, 201
Serial Skepticism, 103
service contracts, 199–200
shelter magazines, 26
SKU data, 196–97
Smith, Mary. *See* Mary
Smith's
snail-mail marketing, 68, 69
special offers, 149
Stark & Stark, 73
strategic context, 14
Super Bowl XXXIV (2000),
123–24
swarming, 25–26, 44–45,
63

ABOUT THE AUTHOR

Mark Stevens, president of MSCO (www.msco.com), is one of the nation's leading experts in ROI-based marketing and the creator of the Extreme Marketing process. Stevens is an entrepreneur, advisor, business builder, and author of such prominent books as *The Big Eight, Sudden Death: The Rise and Fall of E. F. Hutton,* and *Extreme Management.*